Vishwa Mohan Bhatt

♪ The Musical Messiah ♪

Vishwa Mohan Bhatt

The Musical Messiah

Kanchan Mathur

D.K. Printworld (P) Ltd., New Delhi

Cataloging in Publication Data — DK
[Courtesy: D.K. Agencies (P) Ltd. <docinfo@dkagencies.com>]
Mathur, Kanchan, 1948 -
Vishwa Mohan Bhatt : the musical messiah / Kanchan Mathur.
p. cm.
On the life and achievements of Vishwa Mohan Bhatt, Indian classical musician.
ISBN 8124603332

1. Bhatt, Vishwa Mohan, 1951? — Criticism and interpretation. 2. Musicians — India — Biography. I. Title.

DDC 780.92 21

ISBN 81-246-0333-2
First published in India

Published and printed by:
D.K. Printworld (P) Ltd.
Regd. office : *'Sri Kunj'*, F-52, Bali Nagar
New Delhi - 110 015
Phones : (011) 2545-3975; 2546-6019; *Fax* : (011) 2546-5926
E-mail: dkprintworld@vsnl.net
Web : www.dkprintworld.com

To

My Parents

Late Shri G.D. Mathur

&

Smt. Lakshmi Mathur

Preface

THE creator of Mohan Veena and the Winner of a Grammy Award, Pandit Vishwa Mohan Bhatt is an instrumentalist who needs no introduction. He is an artist who has attracted the attention of the world by his Indianization of the Western Hawaiin Guilar.

Mohan Veena, is an eclectic synthesis of the techniques of the Sitar, Sarod and Veena. Pandit Bhatt has given it a revolutionary design and a new tonal fabric by adding 14 more strings. He plays the instrument with blinding speed and a faultless legato-incorporating the gayaki anga with the tantrakari anga.

Pandit Bhatt's quest for the best sound quality led him towards the invention of yet another instrument, called the "Vishwa Veena." In this instrument he has incorporated aspects of the Western Harp into the structure of his Mohan Veena.

Hailed as the "King of Indian Slide Guitar," he entertains audiences all over the world with his limitless supply of Indian classical melodies. Listening to his recitals can be an ecstatic experience, for he rakes up the beauty within you, soothes down painful disturbances while attuning you to the waves of pristine music.

Apart from being a star performer, Pandit Bhatt is a master collaborator too. He has recorded several duets (jugalbandies) with performers of various musical streams.

Pandit Bhatt has indeed gone a long way in setting up the trend for therapeutic classical music while adding to the multitudinous and opulent repertory of Indian classical instruments.

Contents

Acknowledgement

I am very grateful to Pandit Vishwa Mohan Bhatt for allowing me to take a peep behind the curtains and mirror his life through the pages of this book. He took out so much time, from his busy schedule, to divulge information about himself and his works.

There were many occasions when he was too busy to spare any time. It was on such occasions, that his elder son Salil, came to my rescue. Without Salil's help, it would not have been possible for me to gather facts and string them together. It would have been an uphill task to track down the milestones on his climb to success. It would have been difficult to fathom the depths of his psyche and draw out inferences regarding his thoughts and beliefs, emotions and aspirations.

It is indeed a rare blessing to have a son as affectionate, supportive and understanding as what Salil is to his father. The percipience he displays of his father's musings and music, vision and dreams is remarkable. I am grateful to him for all his help.

Writing this book was an enriching experience — for here I was interacting with people who were humble and humane, inspite of being talented; touching heights of fame while still remaining firmly grounded in gentility.

Kanchan Mathur

1

The Grammy Award Winner

1ST March 1994 was a day written in gold in the annals of India. It was a day when a *son rose* on the horizon to cast a glow of *mohani* on the entire *vishwa* with the consonance of his composition entitled 'A Meeting by the River' The silver-toned enchanting 'River,' was a confluence of two streams — one meandering melodiously from the East and the other gushing its way, rhythmically from the West. In other words, it was a day when Pandit Vishwa Mohan Bhatt of India, on his Mohan Veena, and Ry Cooder, an American folk guitarist on his bottle-neck guitar, bagged a Grammy Award for having harmoniously blended melodies from the East and West, into a spirited piece of sheer intoxication, and called it 'A Meeting by the River.'

Grammy to the music world is, what Oscar is to films. Winning a Grammy is the highest honour a musician can ever aim at or

With George Harrison after receiving the Grammy

Facing Page: The Grammy Award — which catapulted Pandit Bhatt to the helm of the music world

achieve. But the duo had got it very early in life. Pandit Vishwa Mohan was only 43 years old then.

'Meeting by the River' was recorded in 1992, after which it figured among the top ten of Billboards World Music Chart for nearly 40 weeks. In 1993 the two musicians were informed that their album had been nominated for the Grammy, in the World Music category. This category is considered to be the toughest because of its vast arena. It includes instrumentalists as well as vocalists, from all over the world.

Pandit Bhatt was, however, totally unruffled by the possibility of his being catapulted to the helm of the music world. In January 1994, a member of the Grammy Organizing Committee happened to ring up his residence to inform him that the grand Grammy Function was scheduled to be held on 1st March, 1994 at Los Angeles. Pandit Bhatt was requested to kindly be present. His elder son, Salil had picked up the telephone. The boy was totally ecstatic at the possibility of his father bagging the most prestigious music award in the world.

The venue for the Grammy was later shifted to New York as Los Angeles was at that time reeling under the devastation brought about by a major earthquake. Even New York was not totally free from the hazards of nature. It was hit by a severe snowstorm on the night of the Grammy. In spite of this, there were endless queues of cars creeping towards the Radio Music City Hall, where the function was being held. Thousands of people lined up the motor way, braving the bitter cold, just to get a glimpse of their favourite stars and superstars from the film and music world. Nearly 1.4 billion people in 110 countries tuned in to watch the show on television.

Pandit Bhatt was led to the front row of the glittering hall packed with music enthusiasts and was offered a seat next to Ry Cooder. The lights dimmed and all eyes focused on the splendid stage. The expectancy of the audience was held at bay for some time by a spectacular display of entertaining pageantry. But time kept creeping towards the Grammy finale — the magic moment everyone had been breathlessly waiting for. People wondered which 'stars' would blazon forth in the firmament of world music that year. The compere uttered the words, "The Grammy for the best album of the year in the world music category, goes to . . . ." — this little silent gap, pregnant with suspense, seemed like a life time to Pandit Bhatt.

When the winners names were finally announced the hall began to resound with a thunderous applause. Somehow Pandit Bhatt failed to hear his name being announced. But when he saw Ry Cooder jump with jubilation, his heart too took a leap of joy. He realized that they had finally made it to the top. Was, it a dream or a blessing from God — Panditji wondered! The two musicians hugged each other. As if in a trance, floating on a wave of happiness, the two made their way up to the stage, to receive the award.

Pandit Bhatt was asked to speak a few words on stage. He took this opportunity to thank his fans for their encouraging support,

and thanked his parents and his guru Pandit Ravi Shankar for enabling him to reach these heights of eminence. He felt that this Award was a salute to those ancient rishis, munis and musicians who had originally composed the Indian Classical raags. He felt happy that he had been able to bring glory to the beauty of their achievements in the Western world too.

After the function Pandit Bhatt spent nearly four hours with members of the press. There were numerous photo sessions. The two musicians faced a barrage of questions and the newspapers next day carried raving reviews of their award winning composition. Suddenly they had become the cynosure of all eyes and heroes to millions all over the world.

Savour the moment —
the celebration cake after the Grammy

Later in the evening a celebration was arranged by some Indian friends and fans at the rooftop of the World Trade Center building. The Indian community in America was particularly very happy and proud to have an Indian brother capture the Grammy.

Pandit Bhatt was enjoying himself at the party but a little voice inside, was coaxing him, now and then, to call it a day and go back to the quiet of his hotel room to relax. He was very tired and the very next day, he was to start on a mammoth tour of America and Canada in which he was to visit 42 cities over a short span of two months.

All this while, he had also been longing to speak to his family. Finally he got a chance to ring up home. His younger son Saurabh picked up the receiver. In quiet tones Panditji informed him that he had been awarded the Grammy.

"What Papa, you have got the Grammy and you are speaking as if nothing much has happened!" was the overjoyed Saurabh's reply.

Panditji was celebrating at the top of the world's tallest building but his family, friends and countrymen felt more like being on top of the world. The entire nation was commending the feat of the great musician who had with great humility and perseverance made his way up to this pedestal of honour. The most emotional of all reactions, came from his old and ailing mother. When she heard the news, she joyously picked up a pen and poured out her emotions lyrically thus:

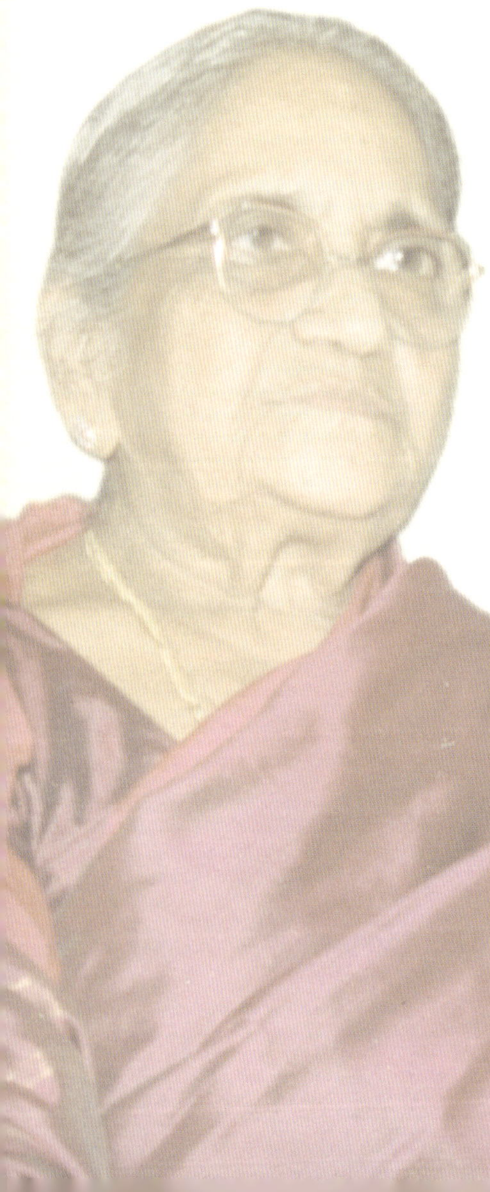

तुझे चांद कहुं या सूर्य कहुं
मेरी आंखों का तारा है
हो जग में रोशन नाम तेरा
बस यही मेरा एक नारा है।

हर देश के कोने-कोने में
तेरी वीणा झंकार रही
भू मंडल से नभ मंडल तक
संगीत की ध्वनि गुंजार रही।

केवल भारत में ही छाई नहीं
यह देश-विदेश में छाई रही
संगीत स्वरों की वर्षा कर
जन-जन के मन को लुभाये रही।

माँ सरस्वती के श्रेष्ठ पुत्र
तुझको माँ ने वरदान दिया
रहे अजर-अमर वीणा तेरी
संसार में जिसने नाम किया।

हो गये धन्य वह माता-पिता
ऐसे सपूत को पाकर के
विश्व ने विश्व को मोह लिया
अपनी मोहन वीणा के तारों से।

श्रद्धा के सुमनों की माला
गुरु-चरणों में अर्पित करना
माँ का है एक उपदेश यही
अभिमान कभी न तुम करना।

जैसे वीणा के तार मधुर
वैसा ही सरल स्वभाव तेरा
जुग-जुग जियो चिर आयु हो
कर रही माँ अभिनन्दन तेरा।

Shall I call you my moon or my sun
You are in fact a star to my eyes
May your name shine in the world
This is the slogan of my life.

The sound of your music
Resounds in each corner of the world
The tinkle of your Veena
Reverberates from Heaven to Earth.

The music of your Veena
Echoes at home and in foreign lands
And it rains nectar
To enchant the entire world.

O! The great son of Goddess Sarasvati
You have been blessed by her
I wish that music of your Veena
May resonate for ever and ever.

How fortunate are the parents
Who gave birth to a son like you
Vishwa you have charmed the vishwa
With the magic of Mohan Veena Strings.

May you always place the garland of respect
At the feet of your esteemed guru
Your mother has only one thing to wish
May arrogant pride never touch you.

Like the sweet notes of your Veena
Your temperament is sweet too
May you live long
Your mother applauds!

With his 95 years old mother Smt. Chandrakala Bhatt

With Pandit Shiv Kumar Sharma

The mother is no poetess, but the beautiful words just flowed out of her heart, so naturally. In fact, she had been very excited even before the Award was announced. Due to over-excitement her nose started bleeding heavily and she had to be hospitalized.

Padma, Pandit Vishwa Mohan's wife, had been worrying so much about her mother-in-law's health, that when Saurabh rang her up to inform her about the award, she was for a moment tense, not wanting to get any bad news about her mother-in-law. She was so relieved and overjoyed when she heard that her husband had been awarded the Grammy.

Streams of friends, relatives and admirers poured in at the Bhatt's residence to congratulate the family. Another person who was really glad was Pandit Ravi Shankar. He was happy that the second Indian to get the Grammy, after he won the honour years ago, was none other than his own shishya — Pandit Vishwa Mohan Bhatt.

The Grammy Award had a very strong impact on the world's attitude to Indian classical music. So far Indian classical music lay oyestered in a shell. Only a small section of music lovers and trained musicians understood its intricacies and appreciated its beauty. To Panditji goes the credit of bringing it out of its shell and taking its pristine appeal to laymen all over the world. Indian classical music is now considered to be a universal language which can touch the emotional depths of even those who do not understand its laws.

♪ 2 ♪

The Lineage

WHILE first approaching Pandit Vishwa Mohan's residence in the Bapu Nagar area of Jaipur, I was overcome by a strange feeling that some invisible ripples of pristine music were gently engulfing me in an effort to purify the soul. This fascinatingly mysterious sensation could have sprung from the fact that here, in this very house, several renowned musicians, through the ages, had created euphonious waves on the sublime ocean of music.

Pandit Bhatt's family has a 500 years old musical tradition. His ancestors belonged to the Telangana region of Andhra Pradesh, in south India. They were brahmana priests who composed and sang songs in praise of

Pt. Manmohan Bhatt and Smt. Chandrakala Bhatt — The proud parents

The family affair — with his father on the harmonium, elder brother Ravi Mohan on the *tabla* and sister on the *tanpura,* while he plays the Violin

the deities. At times their songs reflected man's expectations from God while at other times expressed his longing for communion with God. Mandan, one of Pandit Bhatt's ancestors, was honoured with the title "Kavivar," literally meaning "King of all poets."

At the time when the Kachhawa rulers were laying down the foundation of Jaipur City, a team of eminent poets and musicians was touring the Indian states entertaining the *raja*s and the public. The leader of the team was Shri Vallabhacharya, a renowned poet of the Bhakti Cult. Carrying forward the traditions set by Akbar (the Mogul Emperor, who deeply valued art and culture), the Indian *raja*s in those days made great efforts to draw the best artists and musicians to their courts.

When the team led by Shri Vallabhacharya reached Jaipur, the then Maharaja of Jaipur was so impressed by their artistic talents that he requested some of them to stay back. He felt that their presence would enhance the prestige of his court and enrich the cultural fabric of the state.

Among the artists who accepted this royal invitation was Pandit Kalyan Rai Bhatt, an ancestor of Pandit Vishwa Mohan Bhatt. Pandit Kalyan Rai was accorded a grand welcome by the *Raja* of Jaipur. He was presented huge *jagir*s and a large mansion near Chaura Rasta, one of the main arteries of Jaipur city. The lane where the mansion stood was renamed 'Bhatton-ki-Gali,' literally meaning 'the street of the Bhatts.' Pandit Vishwa Mohan still holds a partial possession of the mansion.

A procession with Pandit Kalyan Rai seated on a royal elephant was taken through the town. Later the same elephant along with a *bagghi* pulled by a pair of horses was presented to the family. The successive generations of the family cherished this *bagghi* very much. Pandit Vishwa Mohan clearly remembers his evening rides on the *bagghi*. He remembers the rhythmic tapping of the horses' hooves, which according to him were one of his earliest lessons in music.

The Bhatt family continued to play an active role in the cultural currents of the state in times to come. Pandit Manmohan Bhatt, the father of Pandit Vishwa Mohan Bhatt, was not only a renowned vocalist but was also well-known for his talent in the field of drama. He acted in and directed several plays, the famous amongst which were 'Hazaar Hath' and 'Ishwarmati.' These plays ran to full houses for several weeks.

To Pandit Manmohan Bhatt goes the credit of having organized the first ever, highly successful marathon music Conference of Rajasthan. Renowned artists like Vinayak Rao Patwardhan, Narain Rao Vyas, Shri Vishnu Digamber Paluskar and V.G. Jog took part in the conference. The public responded to it with great enthusiasm.

Pandit Manmohan Bhatt wanted to popularize Indian classical music. With that aim in mind, he set up the 'Sangeet Kala

Guiding his sons

The fond Guru with his favourite vocalist disciple — Mahalaxmi Shenoy

The *guru* and the *shishya* — none other than his own son Salil

Blessing Salil

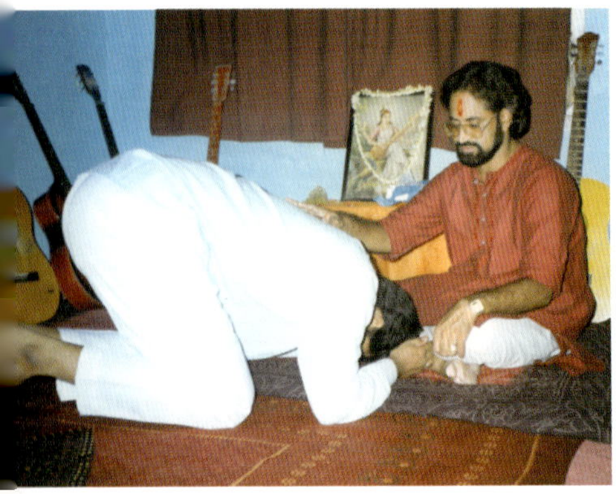

Facing Page: Salil with father, friend, philosopher and guide

Niketan' in 1940. The institute attracted students from different parts of India as well as abroad. Its system of education was based on the ancient Indian *guru-shishya-parampara*. According to the *parampara* (tradition), the *shishya* (student) came to reside with the *guru* (teacher), who in turn imparted education and training to the *shishya* with love. No fee was ever charged. The institution was housed at Pandit Bhatt's residence in Bhatton-ki-Gali. Later in 1961, when the family shifted to Bapu Nagar, the institute also shifted to their new place.

Smt. Chandra Kala Bhatt, the wife of Pandit Manmohan Bhatt was an accomplished vocalist and helped her husband in running the institute.

Sangeet Kala Niketan continues to run even to this day, according to the norms of the ancient *guru-shishya-parampara*, under the tutelage of Pandit Vishwa Mohan Bhatt. The students who pass out from this institute carry their own musical identity. At the institute they are imbued with the sensibility to perceive the temper of different notes, rhythms and their combinations, and are enabled to render them with pinpoint accuracy.

According to Smt. Chandra Kala Bhatt, it takes at least ten years to attain an in-depth knowledge of music — "Only after this lengthy *sadhana* (practise) can one be considered accomplished enough to perform in public." The students who pass out from Sangeet Kala Niketan are successful because they do not have to worry about the burden of tuition fees. They are therefore, free to devote adequate time to the learning process. According to Pandit

Vishwa Mohan, "success in music cannot come instantly. It is a long journey where with every *raga* one gets a drop from an ocean."

Manmohan Bhatt and his wife had always dreamt that their children would also be accomplished musicians. Fortunately, their dreams came true. Their eldest son, Pandit Shashi Mohan Bhatt was a renowned sitarist and a favourite student of Pandit Ravi Shankar. In fact, he was amongst the first three students of the *sitar* virtuoso. The second son, Mahendra Bhatt is a renowned violinist and is attached to the All India Radio. The third son, Pandit Ravi Mohan Bhatt is also a violinist. Their daughter Manju Mehta is a sitarist who is constantly globe-trotting, holding audiences spell-bound with the magic of her music. She runs a music academy in Ahmedabad by the name of 'Saptak.'

Pandit Manmohan Bhatt's youngest son — Pandit Vishwa Mohan's life is, of course, an immortal saga, to whom goes the credit of having invented the Mohan Veena — an Indianized Guitar.

Pandit Vishwa Mohan Bhatt's sons, Salil and Saurabh, are his foremost disciples and are maintaining the family tradition by enthralling audiences all over the world, with their accomplished renderings of Indian classical *raags*.

Salil, the elder son, has a Masters Degree in music and an A-grade of the All India Radio. He is a regular performer at the All India Radio and for the national television network.

Facing page: With younger son Saurabh who is already a successful composer

As a child Salil was attracted more towards acting and sports. Aware of his good looks he had toyed with the idea of acting in films. Later, he went on to qualify for the Indian Military Academy. But his musical genes were too strong to allow him to do either.

He opted for music and got totally immersed in it. Today music is his passion. During his early years of playing the instrument, he kept himself under the shadows of his father, but would be terrified if asked to perform with him. Gradually, as he mastered the instrument his fear faded. He began to discover his own musical identity. He evolved his own style and carved out a niche for himself in the world of music.

Pandit Vishwa Mohan's style of playing the instrument is more serene with an emphasis on the *gayaki anga*. Salil's style on the other hand is more oriented towards the *tantrakari anga*. While playing he displays a superb command over his instrument — with an unfaltering accuracy of notes, a sense of *shruti-laya* and *raag bhava*. His *veena* style *meends*, display a soulful sensitivity towards musical expressions. He enthuses his music with a rare verve while playing his high speed *taans*. Therefore, Salil's music is soulful as well as vibrant.

Referred to as the 'Prince of Raag' and 'the rising son' by the press, Salil has been a celebrity artist on various television channels. His music albums,

Filial bonds — Saurabh with Salil

Facing page: A chip of the old block — grandson Satvik with his 30 inch long replica of the Mohan Veena.

Inset: Wonder kid Satvik and Granddaughter Satkriti

'Revival of Gavti', 'In Harmony', 'Swar Shikhar', etc., have been instant hits.

At such a young age he has already been the recipient of quite a number of awards such as, 'The Mahakal Sangeet Ratna', 'Abhinav Kala Samman', 'Raag Bhavishya', and the 'International Young achiever's Award'. He has been enthralling audiences all over India and abroad — having played in countries like the USA, Ireland, England, Wales, Scotland, UAE, Germany, Switzerland, Italy and Austria.

Saurabh, the younger son, has also gone through an intensive training in Indian classical music. He possesses an instinctive knowledge of the various beats and creates beat patterns that baffle musicians twice his age.

Being rooted so deeply in soulful music, he is now a professional composer. In his compositions the emphasis is on the melody rather than on the beat. These soulful compositions often remind one of R.D. Burman's melodies.

Saurabh's compositional imagination took to wings under the guidance of his father. He assisted his father in composing music for 'Meghadootam', 'Geeta-Govindam', 'Music for Relaxation' and 'Music for Soul'.

At the age of 21 Magnasound signed up Saurabh as a composer and released his first album, *Kaisa Yeh Jadoo*. It is considered to be one of the most melodious and soulful albums of the time. The album is garnering rave reviews from the

Younger son — Saurabh

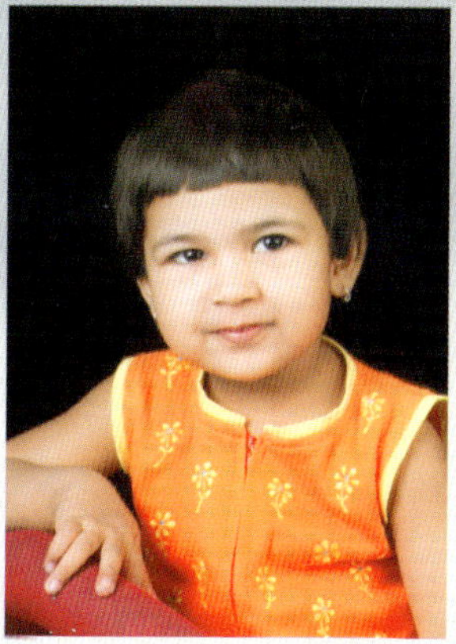

connoisseurs and has caught up the imagination of the common listener too. He has also composed the lyrics and music for a patriotic song on the request of the government of Rajasthan.

Ekta Kapoor of Balaji Telefilms, one of the topmost banners in the electronic media, has invited Saurabh to provide the title and background scores for her serials *Kavita, Kali Re, Karma* and *Kammal*. She likes his music so much that she uses bits of it in her other serials too.

Vinod Rathod has sung some of Saurabh's compositions for a detective serial to be aired on Zee T.V. Saurabh already has a collection of 500 compositions to his credit — a number that belies his age. He has vowed to bring back sheer melody to instrumental music through his compositions. He is very passionate about his XP-80 Roland keyboard, his Spanish guitar and an old tape recorder in which he records his lyrics and musical compositions while sitting up through the night.

Pt. Vishwa Mohan's grandson Satvik (Salil's son) is also showing signs of being a chip of the old block. Even when he was just two years old he could recognize rhythm patterns like *Teen Taal, Ek Taal, Rupak Taal, Jhap Taal, Deep Chandi Taal* and *Keherva Taal*. He was familiar with the names of *raags* like *Madhuwanti, Rageshwari, Yaman, Gavati, Nat Bhairava, Bageshwari, Bihag* and *Sarang*. He could recite the basic notes of *Raag Madhuwanti, Gavati* and *Rageshwari*. He could also recognize the position of notes on the harmonium and could even play the instrument. He was clever enough to recognize and

Facing page: It seems like the musical stream in the family will flow on and on — with son Salil and grandson Satvik

differentiate between the Mohan Veenas of his grandfather, father Salil and uncle Saurabh — even in photographs. Satvik owns a replica of the Mohan Veena, which measures 30 inches, — nearly one-third the length of the original model. He learnt to play the *saptak* on it.

By the time he was three years old he could recognize and name nearly sixty *raags*. His name figured in the *Limca Book of World Records* as the youngest Mohan Veena player.

Satkriti, Satvik's younger sister, who is just three years old, displays her love and sensitivity towards classical music by listening in rapt attention whenever her father Salil performs on stage. She attempts to identify classical *raags* and *taals* and insists on knowing who the *tabla* player is.

It seems like the musical stream in the family will flow on and on, ever-widening with the passage of time to engulf deeper, multitudinous musical currents.

Pandit Bhatt with grandson Satvik and his jing-bang

The famous duo Pandit Bhatt at a function to felicitate Satvik

3

The Early Days

1951 was a momentous year in the life of Smt. Chandra Kala Bhatt, the mother of Vishwa Mohan Bhatt. During this period she was busy, fathoming the waves of Indian classical music, to acquire a Bachelor's degree in music from St. Marie's College, Lucknow. The vibrations of music, which she experienced during this period, were also shared by a little life she nurtured within herself — that of baby Vishwa Mohan. So it can easily be presumed that Pandit Vishwa Mohan took his initiating lessons in music in the mother's womb.

When Smt. Chandra Kala Bhatt sang *lori*es (lullabies) the angels of melody carried baby Vishwa, to a peaceful world of blissful slumber. Probably these early experiences went a long way in crystallizing, for Pandit Vishwa Mohan, an attitude to music — in which music was the path leading to the attainment of peace and communion with God. According to Panditji his mother made him drink music in the form of *ghutti* (a health drink for babies).

His father, Pandit Manmohan Bhatt, had under his tutelage

The Gandha Bandhan ceremony in which Pandi

Posing with the Craftsman, which inspired him to craft the Mohan Veena

students of all religions, castes and creeds. So from a very early age Vishwa Mohan learnt to respect different religions and cultural streams. At that time, every corner of the Bhatt residence was sanctified by the cadence of melody. Growing up in such an environment, the boy imbibed the intoxication of rhythm and melody very early in life. At an extremely young age he began playing musical instruments by the ear. Some of the students of his father were slow learners and lessons had to be repeated for them. Panditji chuckles humorously saying, "I too benefitted from these repetitions."

When Pandit Manmohan Bhatt sang songs, young Vishwa was able to sing back the melodies with utmost accuracy. The happy parents began to feel that some day their child would attain great success in the field of music.

In spite of all his talents, young Vishwa Mohan was a humble, quiet and peace-loving child. He spent all his time after school, toying with the musical instruments lying at home. He never felt the urge to run to the playground. Rather he found enough

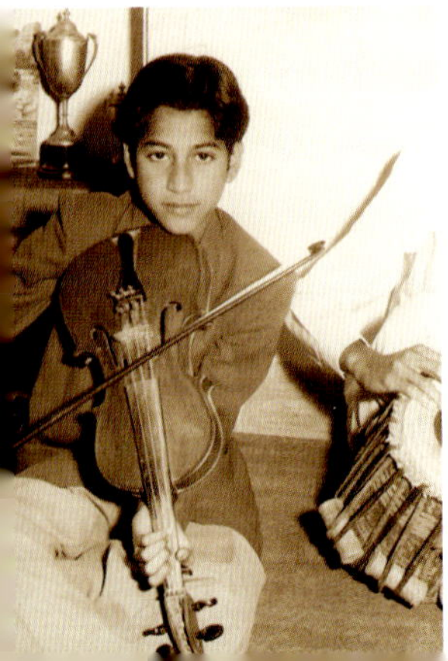

Reveling on the waves of music as a young boy

vi Shankar accepts Pandit Vishwa Mohan as his *shishya*

Talented, yet quiet and humble — the young Vishwa Mohan in 1963

excitement in reveling on the waves of music, in the privacy of his room.

Everyday the students of Sangeet Kala Niketan, irrespective of their religion, gathered to pray to Goddess Saraswati — the Hindu Goddess of music and learning. Young Vishwa never failed to join them in their prayers. He would kneel in front of the Goddess and beseech her to grant him musical talents. He wished that some day he too would become as gifted as his parents and elder brothers.

The innovative streak was always very strong in Vishwa Mohan. As a small boy he once devised his own version of a *bioscope*. He cut out pictures from magazines, stuck them on to a long black strip of paper and then with a torch in hand ran up to invite his grandparents, parents, uncles, aunts, brothers and sisters for a show. The amused audience was led into a darkened room where under torchlight, the boy, kept sliding the black strip, while singing appropriate songs in his childishly sweet voice. The small gathering was amused to no ends by the performance.

While his mother was cooking in the kitchen, young Vishwa

Toying with the Guitar

Mohan would pick up a few steel bowls and fill them up with different amounts of water to get the seven notes of music. He would then enjoy playing on this musical *Jaltarang*.

It was his father, Pandit Manmohan Bhatt, who formally initiated his son to the realm of Indian classical music. He spent long hours daily, imparting knowledge and training in vocal music, while elder brother Shashi Mohan helped Vishwa Mohan acquire proficiency on the *sitar*.

Pandit Vishwa Mohan shared a very special relationship with his father. To him his father was not only his music *guru* but was also his spiritual *guru*. The two often communicated with each other through the language of music. This deep musical communion added depth to their relationship, which became richer and richer with the passage of time.

Pandit Manmohan Bhatt was a great disciplinarian too. The disciplined manner in which Pandit Vishwa Mohan conducts his busy life and the discipline which is reflected in his music is a result of the training received from his father. His seriousness towards musical pursuits is an asset, which he inherited entirely from his father.

Today Pandit Manmohan Bhatt is no more, but the haunting freshness and strength of their relationship has still not diminished. Even today when life weaves a tangled web of problems and Panditji is perplexed, he looks up to his father in heaven for help and guidance. The precepts, embedded in the

Blessings from the
esteemed Guru

fabric of his psyche by his father, rise up to unravel the knotty problems of life.

Whenever Panditji is slightly confused about the expression of a *raag*, he looks up to his father, who guides him towards a better understanding of the *raag*. Panditji observes, "I get a better vision of the *raag* I want to discover. I witness the unfolding of the *raag* and absorb the essence of it for ever." Panditji feels that the deep relationship he shared with his father was a gift from Goddess Saraswati. Recalling his father Panditji says, "My father was my first *guru*. He taught me the basics and essence of music. I was in my late twenties when he left for his heavenly abode. Somehow, I always wanted to converse with him and learn the musical mysteries, but this conversation came to a halt after his demise. Slowly and steadily I got immersed in music. At the same time my desire to have a contact with my father empowered me to establish an unheard dialogue between him and myself."

A life-sized portrait of Pandit Manmohan Bhatt adorns a wall in Pandit Vishwa Mohan's drawing room. He is often found gazing at the portrait. The onlooker can, at that time, sense a deep communion between the two souls. The dialogue, however, is so private that none can guess what it is all about.

Pandit Bhatt clearly remembers old Ashique Hussain Khan Sahib of Ajarada *gharana* who used to visit the Bhatt residence daily to play the *tabla*. He would make the children practice different kinds of beats. The experience left an indelible mark on Panditji's talent.

"You are my inspiration" — with Pandit Ravi Shankar

Pandit Bhatt later became a very special disciple of Pandit Ravi Shankar and remained under his guidance for over nine years. Pandit Ravi Shankar was as keen to guide Vishwa Mohan as the disciple was to be guided. The *guru* had once remarked, "It is indeed a great pleasure for me to impart *talim* of Maihar *gharana* to Vishwa Mohan Bhatt . . . I wish him all success." When Pandit Bhatt went to Pt. Ravi Shankar for guidance he was already an established artist and had successfully invented the Mohan Veena. The training he received from Pandit Ravi Shankar involved intensive and deep discussions about the various Indian *raags* — popular as well as uncommon, and how to render their essence so as to bring out their moods effectively. His proximity to the *sitar* maestro also encouraged him to expose his talents worldwide.

Laying flowers before the life-sized photograph of his father in his drawing room

4

The Avant Garde Innovator

It is all a checker-board of Nights and Days
Where Destiny with Men for pieces plays;
Hither and thither moves, and mates, and slays,
And one by one in the closet lays.

— **Edward Fitzgerald**

FATE had destined Pandit Vishwa Mohan Bhatt to absorb the consonance of divine music and to resonate its vibrations in the *vishwa*. Apart from blessing him with a family, which was totally involved in musical pursuits, destiny seemed to guide his each step towards the attainment of a divine musical goal.

When Panditji was barely 13 years old he acquired a Spanish guitar from a German lady. This was the beginning of his journey towards the evolution of the Mohan Veena — the Indianized version of the guitar.

The German lady was in India to study Indian classical music at the University of Rajasthan. She often visited the Sangeet Kala Niketan to gather knowledge about the intricacies of Indian classical music from Pandit Manmohan Bhatt. At the end of her term, when she was leaving for her homeland, Pandit Manmohan

Bhatt requested her to sell her Spanish guitar to his institute. The guitar was sold for a mere Rs. 25.

It was placed on a shelf in a corner of young Vishwa Mohan's room. The boy who was always attracted towards Western instruments, found this guitar totally irresistible and started fiddling with it. Noticing his son's fascination for the instrument, Pandit Manmohan Bhatt encouraged him to play Indian classical *raags* on it.

Soon, Pandit Vishwa Mohan was playing the instrument very seriously. At the tender age of 15, he gave a public performance on this guitar — a performance which brought him name and fame.

As his involvement with the guitar deepened, he began to feel that the instrument in its original form was not suitable enough to express the intricacies of Indian classical *raags*. He felt that a little modification brought into its structure could evolve special effects suited to conveying the nuances of Indian classical repertoires more effectively.

So he walked up to a shop selling musical instruments near his house and requested Mahavir, the owner of the shop to remove the strings from his guitar and replace them with the strings of the *sitar*. Mahavir was horrified. He thought the boy was out of his mind and told him to go back home and play the *sitar*.

Panditji came back home, but the desire to change the strings did not allow him to sit still. He took a hammer and some nails and with his own hands set about replacing the strings. He removed all

The front view of Mohan Veena

the original strings and fixed three main strings (*sa*, *pa*, *sa*), two drone strings, one *chikari* string and one higher *chikari* string.

He played this instrument till he was 16 years old. All this while, more innovative ideas kept entering his mind. He again began to feel the urge to add on more strings. So he again picked up some nails, a hammer and tuning pads, and attached four *tarab* strings.

Noticing his frenzied fascination for the guitar, his sister Manju Mehta, bought for him a very expensive and sophisticated guitar, on one of her concert tours abroad. The new guitar called 'Craftsman' cost Rs. 25,000 exactly 1000 times more than the cost of the German lady's guitar purchased seven years earlier.

Now, Panditji wanted to remodel the Craftsman too. But this guitar was very expensive and he did not want to handle the remodeling himself. So he contacted Mahavir, the *Sitar* repair expert, he had contacted earlier. He showed him the remodeled version of the German lady's guitar and requested him to bring about identical changes in the Craftsman. Mahavir was also directed to add 8 more sympathetic strings and two *chikari* strings. Once the instrument was ready, Panditji happily played it for a number of years.

But destiny had to lead him further on. He again started dreaming of a sound quality for his instrument, which would be strong and vibrant. He wanted to incorporate into his instrument the depth of *sarod*, the sharpness of *sitar* and the techniques of playing *veena*. In fact, it was the *Vichitra Veena* of north India and

The back view of the Mohan Veena

Pandit Bhatt plays on a stage which is always higher than the seating area of the audience, because he considers his instrument to be a form of goddess Saraswati

the *Gottuvadyam Veena* of south India, which had initially inspired Pandit Bhatt to modify the slide guitar. Panditji felt that by merging the sounds, concepts and techniques of the three older instruments, he could evolve an Indian version of the slide guitar.

Dreams and desires were soon translated into concrete action. He contacted Mahavir who along with Bhaba Sindhu Biswas of Calcutta set about transforming the Craftsman. Pandit Bhatt's residence was the site of this remarkable craftsmanship. Panditji used to sit for long hours supervising the changes. Very often they would skip their lunch too. But Panditji was very particular that his instrument should be handled with care and modified exactly the way he wanted it to be. He doesn't hesitate to add with a smile, "I am a very possessive person. I am very possessive about my instrument and my wife. . . . So I was there with Mahavir and Bhaba Sindhu Biswas all the time."

Under Pandit Vishwa Mohan Bhatt's guidance, the two experts fixed three melody strings mounted on what would be considered the treble side of the neck and four drone strings were fixed coming off the peg-head on the bass side. They were kept lower than the melody strings to facilitate unrestricted playing of the melody strings.

Initially two types of wires were used — straight steel ones and pre-wound ones. The straight wires were used for the first three main strings and the pre-wound ones were used for the last four strings. But Panditji realized that the pre-wound wires were producing a kind of frictional sound due to the sliding of steel bar

In a trance

on it. The sound was not at all melodious. In fact, it was more of a noise. Moreover the pre-wound wires did not give much resonating continuity to sound and the slightest of pressures changed the tension and position of notes. So the pre-wound wires were again changed to straight ones. Twelve sympathetic strings were fixed to yet another level underneath the melody and drone strings, over the fingerboard.

Sitar picks were to be worn on the middle and index fingers and a banjo thumb pick was to be worn on the left hand of the player while a polished rod was to be used as a slide by the right hand to create sound.

And thus a new instrument with a unique tonal fabric was born in the year 1988, adding to the multitudinous and opulent repertory of Indian musical instruments. Panditji happily recalls, "I will never forget the moment when this instrument took on its independent new form. I was immensely happy then. My dream was fulfilled."

This new instrument was capable of creating the grandeur of all the different Indian classical *raags* perfectly. Being an eclectic synthesis of *sitar*, *sarod* and *veena*, it had taken the best qualities of the parent instruments, while improving upon their drawbacks. The resonating continuity of sound after a single strike was so long that as many as 32 notes could be played before the next strike. Therefore there was tremendous scope for the *meend* and the sweep (*ghaseet*). The instrument was extremely suitable for playing the *gayaki anga* as well as the *tantrakari anga*. All the attributes and virtues of the human voice had been skillfully reincarnated into the sound quality of the Mohan Veena. Its light weight and small size enabled the modern day roving musician to carry it around with ease.

The instrument was named Mohan Veena. Mohan is the middle name of Pandit Bhatt and *veena* is an instrument which is played by Goddess Sarasvati. According to Panditji this name struck him when he was immersed deeply into playing a morning *raga*. He recalls, "There was absolute silence and I could imagine that my instrument was producing a sound which I had never heard before. I was playing a certain phrase and I could hear not only what I was playing but could also hear what would come next. I could feel that I was playing things which I did not know, notes that I had never played before. This was the first time I felt a sense of God's presence near me. I could feel God's blessings which were coming in the form of musical notes.

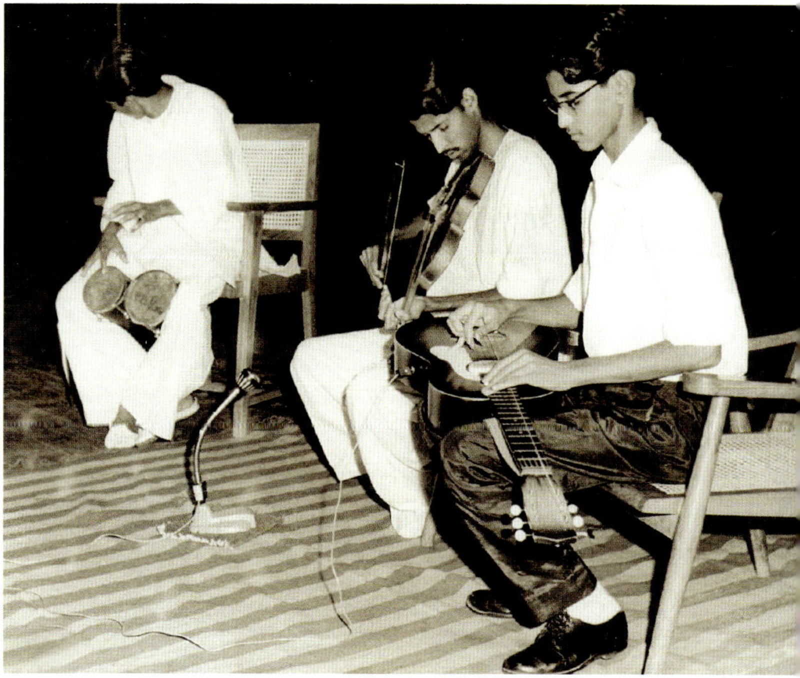

Pandit Bhatt gave his first public performance at the tender age of 15

Mohan Veena has a curved spruce top, mahogany back and sides, a mahogany neck and a flat fretless rosewood fingerboard. It resembles the hollow-bodied curved-top Jazz guitars of the 1920s, which had F-shaped sound holes. It projects sound with great clarity over a long distance. According to the renowned guitar manufacturer and music-critic Rick Turner, "The `Mohan Veena' is under tremendous tension. I would estimate the total string pull to be in excess of 500 pounds. Due to this high tension, the tone turns incredible, with the sympathetics ringing out and strengthening each note played. This is a loud instrument made to cut through in situations with low amplification."

The world welcomed this revolutionary breakthrough in the field of music with great enthusiasm. The press in India and abroad published numerous articles and pictorial representations of the various stages, which had gone into the evolution of the instrument.

The Jawaharlal Nehru Advanced Scientific Research Centre in Bangalore presented to him the prestigious "Musical Scientist Award" at a glittering ceremony at the J.N. Tata Auditorium. Presenting the Award the Centre's president, Mr. C.N.R. Rao, described Pandit Bhatt's innovation as a revolutionary breakthrough in the field of Indian classical music. The award carried Rs. 25,000 in cash, a momento and a certificate. Pandit Bhatt also performed on the occasion amid thunderous applause from the audience.

Mohan Veena is now poised to gain tremendous proliferation and popularity. It is being manufactured in Calcutta, India. This is the city where the best musical instruments, be they guitar, *sitar*, *sarod* or *tabla* are manufactured. To cater to the demands of disciples abroad, the instrument is also being manufactured in Los Angeles, USA.

Pandit Bhatt is very sentimental about his instrument. He, therefore, does not like anyone else touching it. When he goes abroad people are very curious about the instrument and like to touch it. Panditji stops them from doing so by humbly saying, "Please do not touch it, I will tell you all you want to know about it."

He feels the instrument is a delicate piece and can break easily if mishandled. Very often while travelling, the airport staff handle it roughly and it then has to be repaired very carefully.

This happened once when he was to give a performance in Montreal. After reaching the city he realized that a joint on the fingerboard had opened up. He was terribly worried and immediately rung up Rick Turner, the renowned guitar manufacturer in Los Angeles. He was relieved to hear that the instrument could be repaired in Montreal itself by a very efficient repairer. It took nearly four days for the instrument to be repaired. Panditji used to sit at the repair shop from morning till night supervising the repairs

Pandit Vishwa Mohan is emotionally attached to his instrument because he considers it to be a form of Goddess Sarasvati. He therefore likes to place his instrument at a height and away from shoes. Sometime when the stage is lower than the seating area of the audience, he makes it a point to request the organizers to raise the platform where he would play — only because he does not want Mohan Veena to be placed lower than the audience.

With his Craftsman

REY

♪ 5 ♪

Vishwa Veena

PANDITJI'S quest for the discovery of the best sound quality, and his tireless and relentless efforts led him towards the innovation of yet another musical instrument called the Vishwa Veena. This instrument, although played like the Mohan Veena, goes a step forward by incorporating into its structure the features of the Western Harp, along with those of the Mohan Veena — thus giving it a unique sound quality.

In India the Harp could be identified with the *Svar Mandal* whose galaxy of strings are used by so many vocal musicians to provide a continuous drone support to their vocal renderings.

The Mohan Veena was made up using three kinds of wood, namely, mahogany, pine and rosewood. It, therefore, had joints at the sides, back, top and at the neck. This time Panditji wanted the new instrument to be carved out of a single piece of wood.

He went to Rikhi Ram & Sons at Connaught Place, New Delhi, and requested them to translate his dream into reality. Rikhi Ram are one of India's best musical instrument makers. They, too, were excited at the offer and had full confidence in the experienced

Facing Page: In a Trance

Playing the Vishwa Veena — the instrument which incorporates aspects of the Harp into the structure of the Mohan Veena

guidance of Panditji. So they spared no time in starting off on the project.

A large piece of old, well-seasoned Oakwood was procured to be carved out into the new instrument. To begin with, the entire piece of wood was scraped out hollow from the centre, till it looked like a box. It had virtually no joints. Then they sealed it.

Instead of making sound holes like those on the Mohan Veena, they just made perforations for the sound to filter through. The entire length of the instrument was divided into two sections. The part close to the player as he rests the instrument on his lap, was exactly like the Mohan Veena with its system of 20 strings. The other half, away from the player's body, was the section based on the Harp. It consisted of 15 drone strings which caught the vibrations of the main strings and resonated sympathetically. These extra 15 strings could be classed as sympathetic strings also. But in effect, they are more than mere sympathetic because they are also played manually. That is why their gauge and thickness is more than the sympathetic strings.

A melody played on the Mohan

Veena section of Vishwa Veena could quickly be supplemented by a flood of notes from the Harp section of the Vishwa Veena. Thus the Harp section provides a very good support to the notes being played. It complements and adds mystique to the melody. It provides a continuity of notes. The *raag* being played is thus full of notes without even a single moment left vacant.

The melody just fills up the atmosphere so beautifully. The sound which emanates is very soft, sonorous, rich and deep. It goes best with certain very delicate and subtle melodies.

The instrument is in the final stages of its formation but Panditji still keeps experimenting with it. Sometimes he tries to change the bridges and at times tries to change the arrangement of strings. It has been played in all the major Indian cities and audience have welcomed it and appreciated its sound very much.

The front & back view of Vishwa Veena

Working the magic of strings

6

Music and Baaj

TO Pandit Vishwa Mohan Bhatt, music is *puja*, *aradhana* and *tapasya*. To him it is not merely an act of playing the instrument but is also a means of communication with the cosmic composers. He believes that music is the path leading to the attainment of *moksha* (freedom from birth and rebirth).

"Music is the best way of concentrating and cleansing the soul. . . . It is absolutely *nirmal*, *svachha* (pristine, pure). It is transparent. It purifies not only the singer but the listeners as well. I am thankful to God that I have the talent to understand the language of music," he observes.

During his early years of playing the Mohan Veena, he would rehearse non-stop for the better part of the evening and night. During this period no one was allowed to disturb him — not even for food and water. Probably music was his food for life — so he kept playing on.

Today Panditji is hailed as the 'King of Indian slide guitar' and a 'power house performer whose electrifying performances drive listeners wild'. With his limitless supply of melodies, Panditji has

entertained audiences all over the world. Each time he steps on stage, the audience accord him a hero's welcome. His humble and demure demeanour, however, belies his huge fame.

Listening to Panditji play on his Mohan Veena can be an experience of sheer ecstasy. He brings out the beauty within you, evokes worthy emotions and soothes down painful disturbances, while attuning you to the waves of pristine music. As his music swings from lilting slow to a delirious effervescence, he takes you over an extremely wide tapestry of emotional patterns. His *veena* tugs at your heartstrings and makes them vibrate responsively.

Panditji's style, which he has mastered to perfection, is a blend of the *gayaki anga* (vocal style) and the *tantrakari anga* (instrumental style). In fact, at times it becomes difficult to tell whether he is playing a piece on the Mohan Veena or singing it.

The *gayaki anga* is characterized by longevity and continuity of notes with their smooth interlinking (*legato*). The process involves a skillful use of *meends*, *gamaks* and *ghaseets*. Panditji displays the *gayaki anga* so very beautifully in his *alaps* at the beginning of each of his concerts. The *alap* initially belonged to the *gayaki anga* only but later started getting incorporated into the *tantakari anga*. It is a slow, beatless expansion of the *raag*, in which the musician develops the delicate and intricate nuances of the *raag*. The musician gives a general and total impression of the *raag*, its nature and flow through the various *saptaks*. Through his *alaps*

At the release of the music album of the film Bawander. Pandit Bhatt contributed to its background music

Panditji helps his listeners to get immersed into the purest *raag* mood.

Pt. Bhatt is superb in his delineation of the *pakad*s (idiosyncratic essence of the *raag*) — be it a scintillating rendering of *raag Tilak Kamod* and *Hamsadhvani* or a plaintive and poignant exposition of *raag Bhairavi*. He manoeuvres through the *raag* with fluency and finesse exhibiting a complete command over the *svar*s. He can negotiate the complex transitions from one note to another with complete ease. His renderings display a deep insight into the *raag* structure, highlighted by needle-point accuracy of *laya*.

He also remains unrivalled in his ability to play with blinding speed. His *jhala*s are masterpieces of craftsmanship.

Another praiseworthy feature of Pandit Bhatt's style are his mellifluous *meend*s (glides), played in the style of *veena*. These serpentine *meend*s always receive roaring applause from the audience. The repertoires are sprinkled with enlivening *gamak*s and *andolan*s.

"Sky is the limit for me"
— Vishwa Mohan Bhatt

The *saval-jawab* sessions on the *tabla* are also one of the high points of his recitals. During a *saval-jawab* session the main artist renders a phrase of *svar*s which prolong upto one full sixteen beat cycle. The *tabla* player, who always uses the same number of beats as the main artist, then renders the same phrase. The *tabla* player cannot

"Switch off the salvo of lusty music. It robs music of its delicacy and depth", says Pandit Bhatt

actually play the *svars* but he replicates the exact tone, loudness, stress and longevity of notes, so that it gives the listener the impression that the artists were involved in a *sawal* (question) and *jawab* (answer) session.

Another fascinating effect that Panditji often creates is the echo effect. He creates this effect through tonal and volume modulations. The fade-out of the echo is achieved over two or three repeats, in diminishing volume.

The feature that strikes the audience most is the clarity of his tones. One never hears the sound of the finger picks clashing against metal strings. All one hears is the clean note itself in its purest form. It virtually sounds as if the cosmic consonance was resonating from the heavens above — while the audience sit mesmerized.

Panditji displays tremendous versatility while rendering the *raags*. He skillfully uses forbidden notes to convey poignantly beautiful shades of music. Speaking about his creative imagination he says, "My imagination just overlaps sometimes. I take the liberty to improvise and play whatever is in my imagination — but only within the framework of the *raag*."

'The Son' of India

Pandit Bhatt's performances are so many and at such close intervals that he never really gets much time to prepare in advance. Very often he decides upon the *raag* to be played after reaching the stage. A spiritual force then gradually guides him into the flow of the *raag* and he starts playing it with all the skill and fire of a virtuoso. Fathoming the mysteries of music Pandit Bhatt creates an ambience wherein one loses the sense of the temporal and gets a taste of the spiritual heights of music. At the end of it all the audience is left yearning for more.

One often wonders why Pandit Bhatt had to pick up the guitar to play Indian classical music when there were so many Indian instruments readily available to him. But Panditji wanted to be "one in a thousand." He says, "I wanted to try something unusual. I wanted to contribute something to Indian music." While explaining how he expresses his musical passion on the Mohan Veena, he says, "while I play on it, I find it a completely new instrument each time. . . . It is strange, I keep exploring on the ocean of music through this instrument."

According to Panditji, "When an artist creates his art form, his primary aim is to establish a communion with God. The aim of pleasing or impressing the audience in any particular manner is secondary." But audience response does make a difference to him. He can always feel his audience and feels responsible to give his best to them. He says, "while giving recitals an artist has to keep two things in mind — one is honesty to the classical tradition and second, the responsibility to give the best to the audience . . . All I need is an appreciative audience, a full house, a great acoustic system and excellent air conditioning. The positive response eggs me on to go higher and higher and perform more complicated stuff."

Pandit Bhatt is often referred to as the "King of Fusion Music" for he has very successfully combined with so many musicians from all over the world to create beautiful musical albums. Experimenting with new ideas comes so naturally to Panditji. He says, "it feels good to interact with high calibre players from other musical systems. We can talk to each other through the universal language of music and may be that can help the world go better."

The best part of his fusion music is that he has never allowed the uniqueness of Indian classical music to be lost. The fusions have been achieved without compromising on the individuality of either of the players. Panditji believes that, "In Indian classical music we have scales of every level which can match the music from any part of the world." His fusions are based on this awareness of this greatness of Indian classical music.

The one quality he admires in musicians is originality. "I like artists who have their own originality — who do not get lost in maintaining tradition. For example, Beethoven and Mozart did great things ages back. Pandit Ravi Shankar, Ustad Amir Khan, *kya gana tha unka, mujhey aaj samajh mein aa raha hai* (Now I am beginning to understand what their music was all about). Zakir Bhai does a very good job. I like his presentation very much. It is a golden time for music — but a changing time too. People are creating new things."

But while speaking about the salvo of lusty, thundering clang-clatter-clangour of

music played on some of the satellite TV channels, Panditji feels it has robbed music of its pristine delicacy. He feels "people are now linking music with nudity and sex — it is vulgar and purely commercial." But he humbly adds on, "it may be right in their sense of music."

Pandit Bhatt feels that classical art forms should reach the masses and not just connoisseurs. He often appeals to the corporate sector and commercial houses to take up promotion of fine arts amongst the masses — "It is after all meant for them too."

Panditji was once asked if he would ever take up scoring music for films and he had replied, "I don't think I will. I am not prepared to make compromises in the music I play. May be I might compose film music if I meet a producer who understands the language of music. If someone comes forward to allow me to score music on my own terms and according to my taste then perhaps I might consider."

Probably Panditji did find such an opportunity when he recorded music for ace film director Mani Ratnam's "Anandam" along with the famous music director A.R. Rehman. He has also contributed to the background music of "Bawander."

Hollywood film producers were highly impressed by Pandit Bhatt's music. A portion from "A Meeting by the River" has been incorporated into the background music of Tim Robbin's "Dead Man walking." "Two Days in the Valley," another Hollywood film has used a portion of his fusion music with singer Taj Mahal.

The press has voiced its estimation of esteem for Pandit Bhatt's pristine, pure, delicate yet fiery music in various ways:

1. One of the greatest and most expressive slide players in the world. — *Elijah World*, Acoustics Guitar magazine (USA).
2. Pandit Bhatt is the most popular Indian artist abroad. — *The Hindustan Times*, India.
3. Vishwa Mohan invented "Mohan Veena" to put his stamp on Indian classical music. — Brian Mann, *Columbia Daily Tribune*, USA.
4. Cultural Ambassador of India. — *The Hindu*, India.
5. Vishwa Mohan is an inspiration even to Western guitarists. — Roger Levesque, *Edmonton Journal*, Canada.
6. The Guitar's Indian Avatara (Reincarnation). — *Deccan Herald*, India.
7. A creator of new sounds. — *Gulf News*, UAE.
8. God's Messenger of Indian Classical music. — Prakash Bhandari, *Times of India*.
9. Bhatt is the world music hero. — *Texas Express News*, USA.
10. Bhatt is the guitar man. — Errol Nazareth, *The Toronto Sun*, Canada.

The fan club

7

A Chapter from Mills and Boon

PADMA (née Anne Randell) first met her husband Vishwa Mohan when she joined the Sangeet Kala Niketan to learn the guitar. She had inherited a love for music from her mother who was a very good musician. Mrs. Randell played the piano and the violin very well.

There was a violin lying at home, so she asked her daughter Anne to take up lessons in violin. But Anne's friends were all going to learn the Mohan Veena, and she preferred to learn the same with them.

So Vishwa Mohan started teaching the Mohan Veena to Anne. The young lady was highly impressed by her teacher and his music. At home, during meal times, she would keep talking about the institute, about how good and talented the family was, and most of all, how good her teacher was. The Randell family would listen to these golden opinions without much reaction or comment.

Anne came from a highly westernized and a highly educated Christian family. They followed the Bible

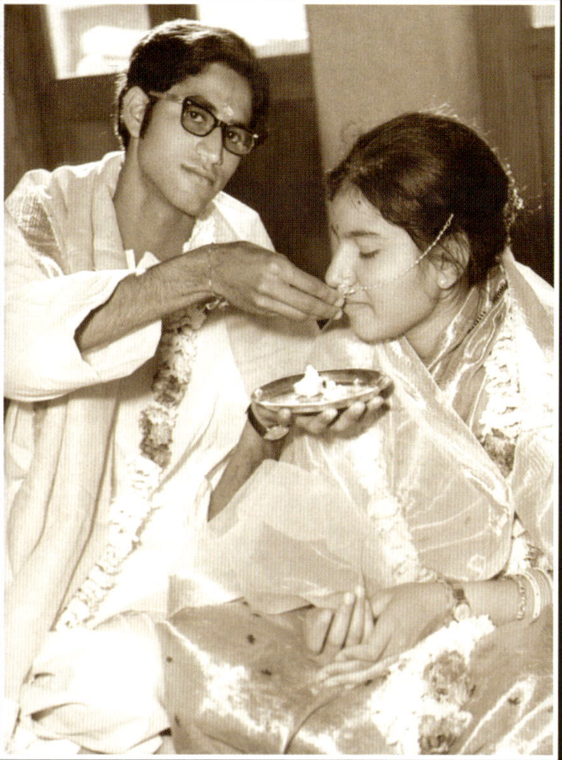

And they lived

happily ever after

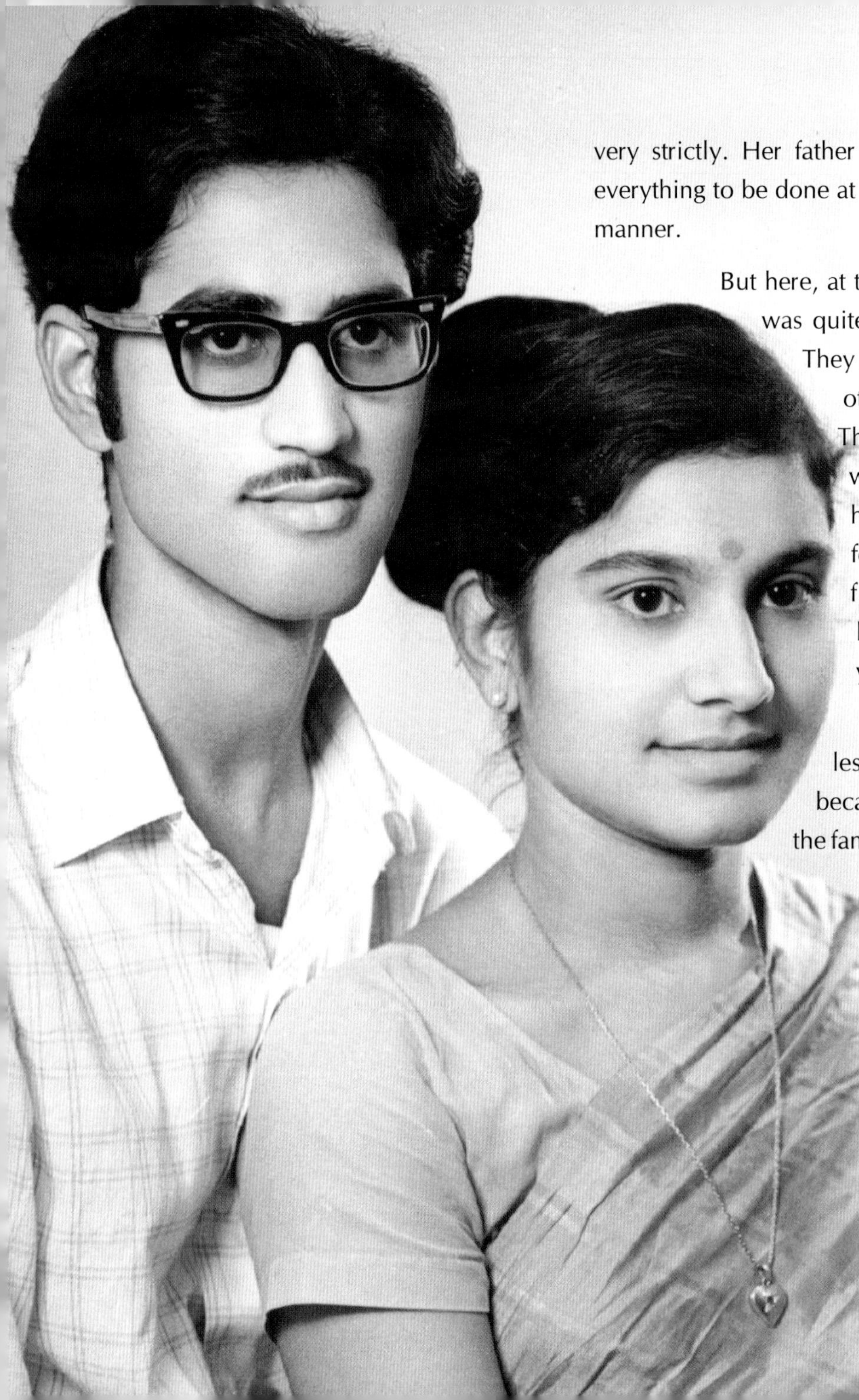

very strictly. Her father was a great disciplinarian who liked everything to be done at the proper time and in the most proper manner.

But here, at the home of the Bhatts, the atmosphere was quite different. People were more relaxed. They had so much love and affection for each other and did not hesitate to display it. They would sit and chat and have tea whenever they liked. In her father's house there were set timings for tea, like for all other things. The Bhatt home was filled with music, happiness and laughter. All this, and more, enamoured young Anne to the Bhatt family.

Anne was not very regular with her lessons. She would often be absent, either because she had examinations or because the family was going out of station on vacation. Once she was away for nearly a month and a half as she had contracted typhoid. Vishwa Mohan was very worried and decided to pay her a visit.

For Anne it was a very pleasant surprise. She did not

really expect him to notice her absence, as there were nearly a hundred students under his tutelage. Besides, she never ever expected him to visit her.

Vishwa Mohan was very expressive about his concern for her. He said to her, "You are looking very weak and you have also lost a lot of hair."

Anne felt shy and wanted to laugh. She had till then not realized that men took notice of things like girl's hair. All the same, she was very happy that day.

Back to the music school, she began to notice that Vishwa Mohan gave her special time and attention. It thrilled her no end. Gradually they both began to realize that their affection for each other was blossoming into love.

Pandit Manmohan Bhatt also noticed this development. He liked Anne a lot. Once he rang up his wife, who was a lecturer at Bharatpur at that time and told her about this lovely young lady who would be just right for their Vishwa Mohan.

Neither of the young people ever proposed to each other, but it was mutually understood that this friendship would end up in marriage. The Bhatt family was prepared for it.

Time flew. Anne finished her graduation, and her parents wanted to

with his wife Padma and his sons Salil & Saurabh

Diwali pujan with his Christian turned Hindu wife

Bonded with love — with wife and son Salil

With Padma at the Sea beach

With wife Padma — the queen of his heart

Happy Moments

"My favourites" — wife, instrument and Pixie

move to Chennai and get their daughter married to a nice south Indian boy. Anne was absolutely scared at the prospect.

Vishwa Mohan was by now so totally enamoured and enraptured by his lady love, that he could just not bear the thought of separation. He would often be caught crying in the privacy of his room.

Anne then decided to tell her parents about Vishwa Mohan. The parents were horrified. Being staunch Christians, how could they allow their daughter to marry a Hindu? They said they liked the boy, but would agree to the marriage only if he converted himself to Christianity. And that was just not possible!

In fact, Anne's great grandfather had been a Hindu *pujari* in Chennai. Those days Christian missionaries were busy converting Hindus to Christianity. They distributed Bibles and preached Christianity to the Hindus at the Marina Beach. Her grandfather was so impressed by the preaching of the Christian missionaries that he converted himself to Christianity. Annoyed by the conversion, the great grandfather brought out a balance. He kept the Bible on one side and a lot of riches on the other, and asked his son to choose between the two. The son chose the former. Since then the family remained true to Christianity.

The Hindu genes, inherited from her great grandfather, were very strong in Anne's blood and she took great interest in the religious rituals performed by her Hindu friends. She was fond of putting *henna* on her palms like the other Hindu girls. She loved wearing bangles and putting a *bindi* on her forehead. She was averse to eating meat. In fact, she just wanted to be the same as the crowd of Hindu girls around her.

Anne was adamant that she would marry Vishwa Mohan. In the end her father could do nothing except accept it as God's will. The Bhatts were very happy with the alliance and decided to get them married according to the *Arya Samaj* rites. Anne was renamed and has since then been known as Padma.

And this was the beginning of a truly happy married life for both of them.

The family photograph — Saurabh, Pandit Bhatt, wife Padma, Salil's wife Preeti and Salil

A *Jugalbandi* with Salil

8

Selected Compositions and Indian Discography

PANDIT Vishwa Mohan will never forget his performance, which took place in Bombay in 1970. Sur Sringar Sansad, an organization devoted to promoting young, talented, budding artists, had organized a show where Panditji was invited to perform along with other artists. This was also Panditji's very first major public performance. He had put in a lot of time and effort in preparing for it. He was newly married and decided to take his wife along with him. They were both so young that the family had to send his elder brother Ravi Mohan as an escort. Vishwa Mohan's soul-stirring performance at the show that day left the audience spellbound and the newspapers next day carried raving reviews.

Shri Mohan Nadkarni, a top ranking music critic attached to *The Times of India* for more than 50 years, was also present at the recital. His review next day carried the caption "A teenager steals limelight." He forecast a glorious future for the youngster. He felt that Panditji had given the guitar a new life. Panditji's son, Salil, has preserved a cutting of that review.

Gold-plated replica of the Mohan Veena presented by the then Chief Minister of Rajasthan Shri Bhairon Singh Shekhawat after Pandit Bhatt received the Grammy

With Late Sri Gulshan Kumar, owner of T Series, for whom he recorded many albums

In January 1997, exactly 27 years later, Panditji again received a letter from Mr. Nadkarni in which he reminded him of the prophecy he had made so long ago — and how very true it had come to be.

Mr. Nadkarni has compiled a directory of eminent Indian musicians — the very first of its kind. Pandit Vishwa Mohan adorns the cover along with Pandit Ravi Shankar, Pandit Bhimsen Joshi and some other eminent artists of yesteryears.

Also present at the Bombay recital in 1970 was Mr. Murli Manohar Swaroop, a composer with HMV, the most prestigious recording company of that time. Mr. Swaroop was so impressed with Panditji's performance, that at the end of the show he went back stage with his HMV colleagues and approached Vishwa Mohan with an offer to record his music. For Panditji it was like a dream come true. He readily and most gladly accepted the offer.

Life's First Recording

So the next day he was at the HMV studio recording the very first disc of his life. Initially he was a little nervous. He had never been inside a recording studio before but was very fascinated by the various recording procedures and recording instruments kept around. Gradually his nervousness began to ease and he started settling down with his instrument. The recordist signalled to him to start — and Pandit Vishwa Mohan was there giving his very best. He played *Rageshwari* on one side of the disc and *Desh* on the other side. Manik Rao Popatkar, a famous *tabla* player accompanied him on the *tabla*. Later a photograph of the young artist was taken to be put on the cover of the disc. The disc was released six months later. Panditji recalls, "that incident is still fresh in my memory and well remain so for ever. After that I must have recorded hundreds of discs but I do not have such a clear memory of these recordings."

This was the first time that a recording of a hybrid instrument such as Panditji's was sold in the market. The public showed great curiosity and appreciation for the instrument, its sound and its artist. The record made big sales in India as well as abroad. It also established Panditji as a professional artist of repute. Panditji recalls, "I was so happy with this record that I loved looking at my photograph and name on the cover and did so ever so often."

Jugalbandi with Late Pandit Shashi Mohan Bhatt

The next disc which Panditji recorded is very dear not only to Panditji but to his entire family as well. In this he has played a *jugalbandi* with his elder brother Late Pandit Shashi Mohan Bhatt, who played the *sitar*. Shashi Mohan is no more and the disc is now a part of the family's treasure.

Shashi Mohan had always been very appreciative of his younger brother's achievements. Pandit Vishwa Mohan Bhatt respected him like a *guru* and a father.

Pandit Vishwa Mohan playing a *jugalbandi* with elder brother Shashi Mohan Bhatt on the *Sitar*

In this *jugalbandi* one can sense a kind of restraint on Panditji's part, because here he was playing with an individual whom he revered and was therefore somewhat reticent with. Still, it is a beautiful *jugalbandi* in which the brothers played *Madhuwanti* and *Hemant*. It was recorded by HMV in 1977.

Those days there was an artist in Bombay who was an expert at making huge idols of Indian Gods and Goddesses with damp sand at the Juhu Beach. He used to colour these sand idols attractively. Visitors at the beach used to bow in front of the idols and make some cash offerings. The artist would demolish the idols after two or three days and make new ones again.

Once he had made a huge idol of Lord Hanuman. That was the day the two brothers happened to be at the beach. They thought it would be a good idea to get themselves photographed in front of the idol and use the picture for the cover of their disc. So they spread out a mat in front of the idol and holding their respective instruments got themselves photographed — a rare picture on a disc cover.

The 1980s

The 1980s list very few recordings of Panditji. During that decade HMV was going through a bad phase in its corporate life and was, therefore, not conducting very many recordings — especially of classical musicians. Besides the HMV, there were other recording companies on the scene, but they were too small in stature to venture into classical music. They were only delving into film and light music.

The Golden Trio

The 1980s also saw the birth and rise of quite a few recording companies. CBS was one such company, which started by recording film music, but by the end of the decade was ready to record classical musicians as well. Panditji recorded two albums for the CBS during this period. In 1988 he recorded an album in which he played *raga Bihag, Nat Bhairava* and a *dhun*. In 1989, he recorded the 'Golden Trio' along with two other artists. In this disc he played *raag Yaman* and *Nat Bhairava* again.

Enchanting Folk Melodies

By 1989 the HMV had started making efforts to struggle back to a revival. They recorded with Panditji a disc entitled "Enchanting Folk melodies." It included melodies from the different states of India.

Galaxy of Strings

T-series that was born in mid 1980s had by 1990 risen on the music horizon like a giant. It had started by recording film music, but by 1990 was well prepared to venture into the classical music arena. Among the first batch of classical musicians it recorded, was Pandit Vishwa Mohan Bhatt. The disc was called 'Galaxy of Strings' named after the 20 strings of the Mohan Veena. Panditji played *raag Hem Bihag, Bageshwari* and a *dhun* in *Pahadi*. The record made booming sales. T-series had priced their cassettes at such economical rates that classical music could now reach a common man's home. Even years after the release of the cassette, its demand in the market is immense.

Recording with Concord

In 1991, Concord, a recording company based in Calcutta recorded a disc with Panditji. The recording studio was small, but what Panditji liked about the place was that they had kept a statue of Goddess Sarasvati there. Panditji felt as if he was playing in a temple. He played *raga Gavti*, *Kirwani* and *Desh*. The disc sold well in the eastern region of India but could not reach the other parts.

Guitar-a-la-Hindustan

In 1992 Pandiji accepted the offer of recording another disc for HMV in which he played *raga Jog*, *Madhuwanti*, *Khamaj* and a *dhun*.

At that stage Magnasound came on the scene in a big way and started recording classical musicians. Panditji recorded a disc with them in 1992. The disc was called 'Guitar-a-la-Hindustan.' The recording was conducted at the Western Outdoor — India's best recording studio in Bombay.

It happened to be Panditji's second recording that day. He had just completed a recording at some other studio and braving the awful Bombay heat had reached the Western Outdoor. He had been extremely uncomfortable, but the comfortable air-conditioned interiors of the studio put him at ease and he got into the mood of playing *Kausikanhra*. It is a deep and serious *raag*, which takes you on an inward journey to rediscovering your soul. It is a *raag* that is not so easy to play and is rarely heard in the concert and recording circuits. Very few eminent artists like Ustad Ali Akbar Khan and Nikhil Banarjee have played it. So Panditji began the cassette with a soul-search and then went on to play *raag Tilak Kamod* — a sweet, scintillating, popular evening *raag*. He ended up by playing *Chandra Kauns* — again a serious night melody. Since Magnasound was associated with the Warner Bros of USA it had a big market potential in the West. The record made very good sales in the East as well as the Western world.

Song of Nature

The very same year came another cassette by Magnasound called 'Song of Nature' in which Panditji had so very beautifully depicted the various moods of nature through the musical language.

Ragas Morning to Midnight

On the same theme, T-Series brought out 'Ragas Morning to Midnight' — and also released it in 1992. Here Panditji played *Hem Bihag*.

In Harmony with son Salil V. Bhatt

Next came a disc, recorded by Crescendo in 1993. The disc was called 'In Harmony with son Salil V. Bhatt'. The practice sessions for this disc were, however, not always very harmonious. Salil, otherwise a highly accomplished artist, was recording a disc with his father for the very first time and was therefore very nervous. Out of nervousness, he kept making

With Ustad Bismillah Khan

the kind of mistakes he never makes otherwise. It infuriated Panditji to see Salil in this state and he scolded him many times.

Finally, Salil decided to revive his self-confidence and fight back his nervousness. Sure enough, the final recording was beautiful. Panditji was also happy with the recording. They played *Bihag*, *Gurjari Todi* and a *Rajasthani dhun* called *Hitchki*.

As a reward Panditji offered Salil some money. In the beginning Salil was hesitant to take it, but finally accepted it, for this was really going to be his first remuneration through music. He used up the entire money to buy copies of the cassette to distribute among his friends, relatives and the artists he admired.

Later, each time Salil heard the recording, he regretted not having played as well as he could have. But Panditji told him that this kind of feeling will beset him each time he did a recording in future too. According to Panditji the deeper one goes into music, the more he realizes his mistakes and shortcomings and tries to rectify them. The day an artist starts feeling that he has done his best and can do no better, his talent starts declining. Panditji feels that the more one achieves, the more dissatisfied he should be, for this is the only way he can accelerate his progress.

In 1993 itself Panditji recorded a *jugalbandi* for Music Today. He played *Gorakh Kalyan*, *Yaman* and a *dhun* in *Maand*.

Geet Govindam

Composing music was also in Panditji's nature. He started his career as a composer in 1994 when he composed music for 'Geet Govindam' — a dance serial telecast on the national network. *Geet Govindam* is an epic poem written in Sanskrit by the famous poet Jaidev.

Shri Karpoor Chand Kulish, the owner of Rajasthan Patrika Ltd., wanted the poem to be choreographed into a dance form. He spent nearly a crore in picturising the dance scenes at various locations in Rajasthan such as Jaipur, Jodhpur and Udaipur. Pandit Vishwa Mohan was invited to compose its music. Those days the studios in Jaipur were not so highly developed and had virtually no provision for track recording. The task of recording was therefore not only difficult but also time consuming. The entire recording took nearly one and a half years to complete.

The music, which Panditji composed, was a fusion of Rajasthani folk and Indian classical music. Along with *sitar*, *sarod*, *santoor* and flute Panditji used quite a number of folk instruments, which were not very commonly heard. Folk artist from the hinterland of Rajasthan — the Langas and the Manganiyars — played the *khartal*, *morchhang*, *sarangi* and *dholak*.

This careful fusion of semi-classical and classical streams conjured up images of a sprawling desert. Its typically rural flavour signified the simplicity and sweetness of the natives of the desert of Rajasthan. It won excellent reviews from the critics and the public loved it very much. 'Geeta Govindam' was telecast on the national network as a 20-episode serial.

With the then Chief Minister of Karnataka, after a concert

Music for Relaxation

Just before bagging the Grammy Pandit Bhatt also composed 'Music for Relaxation' recorded by Music Today. In this album his music was a fusion of the contemporary and the traditional classical music. He used a lot of Western instruments like the keyboard, octapads and drums.

The compositions depicted a wide range of emotional patterns. They depicted feelings at sunset and sunrise and also the feelings of love, loneliness and agony. The music elevated one to the realization of the pristine sublimity of Creation and in the process soothed him. Its musical currents flowed into the deepest recesses of one's heart — evoked emotional reactions, which flowed out sympathetically as catharsis — thus relaxing the listener. He, therefore, named the album 'Music for Relaxation'.

The music took one to meadows where Krishna once played his flute. One moment the listener was hearing the tinkle of the shimmering silver ripples of a rivulet and the next moment he moved into a divine silence, which in itself was so meaningful. Yet again, one rode the crest of a gracefully joyous world, which gradually ebbed into the beauty of pathos. On the whole the music was nothing short of a taste of the elixir. After its release in 1995 it became a rage in the market and kept creating new records all over the world in the coming years too.

Lure of the Desert

In 1994, Panditji recorded 'Lure of the Desert' with T-Series. This was Panditji's first recording after winning the Grammy. T-Series too, was at its peak.

The recording was fixed for 16th June 1994. Just two days earlier Panditji had been bestowed with State honours in his home state of Rajasthan for having bagged the Grammy. At a glittering ceremony at the Birla Auditorium of Jaipur, Panditji had been gifted a cheque of Rs. 1 lakh and a gold plated replica of Mohan Veena by the then Honourable Chief Minister of Rajasthan, Shri Bhairon Singh Shekhawat.

So when he reached the Jaipur Airport to fly out to Bombay for the recording of 'Lure of the Desert', he was thronged by many admirers, seeking autographs. The television at the airport lounge was telecasting a video recording of the previous day's award-giving ceremony. Panditji was really touched and overwhelmed by all this show of affection and public attention showered upon him.

The flight to Bombay was a hopping one with a short stop over at Udaipur. Due to technical reasons it was delayed at Udaipur and Panditji managed to reach Bombay just a couple of hours before the actual recording.

From the airport he drove straight to the Golden Chariot Studio to inspect the recording arrangements. The studio was considered to be one of the largest and the most efficient audio-video recording studios in Asia. Panditji was very happy to see the arrangements there. A part of the studio had been enchantingly

Acknowledging applause

transformed to look like a tiny township of Jaisalmer. There were those typically ethnic mud-houses set up besides the representation of a magnificent *haveli*. The sitting area suggested the undulating sand dunes of the desert.

Shri Gulshan Kumar the owner of T-Series then took him home instead of allowing him to move into a hotel. Gulshan Kumar was a great admirer of Panditji. The artist enjoyed his warm hospitality and after some rest was back at the recording studio.

The entire ambience of the props was so beautiful and the acoustics so correct that Panditji took no time in getting into the perfect mood. Another rare feature about this recording was that both the audio and video recordings were conducted simultaneously. Panditji played *raag Desh, Megh Malhar* and a *dhun* in *Vrindavani Sarang*.

The album was released after four months. It made remarkable sales and continued to feature among the top selling albums for a long time.

Chaturang

1995 was a busy year for Panditji as far as recordings were concerned. He recorded "Chaturang," a cassette for Crescendo, in which he played *Madhuwanti* and *Nat Bhairava*. In another cassette for the Venus he played *Ahir Bhairava* and *Hemant*. Tips recorded a *jugalbandi* in which Panditji played *Rageshwari* with Tarun Bhattcharya.

The Instrumental Trio

HMV released another album with the title Mohan Veena in which Panditji played *Shyam Kalyan* and *Rageshwari*.

HMV also recorded 'The Instrumental Trio' in which Panditji played folk tunes from the different states of India. He also played *raag Hemant* and *Basant* and a *dhun* in *Mishr Bhairavi*.

Maestro's Mehfil, Song of Nature and Romantic Raga

'Maestro's Mehfil' was recorded for the T-Series in which Panditji played *Desh*. Magnasound brought out 'Song of Nature — Part III.' The melodies recorded here were all composed by Panditji himself, in which he used a variety of Western instruments like the rhythm box, electronic keyboard, violin, flute, etc. Music Today released 'Romantic Raga' in which Panditji played a *dhun* in *Mand*.

Vishwa Veena

1996 began with Zee Music's Vishwa Veena in which rare *raags* like *Jogeshwari*, *Jai Jai Vanti* and *Manj Khamaj* had featured. This also happened to be Zee Music's first cassette ever.

The Best of the Chord

The same year the India Music Club, a USA-based organization recorded 'The Best of the Chord' in which Panditji played *raag Gavati*, *Desh*, *Pahadi* and *Bhairavi*. India Music Club had a global reach. Its owner lived in Kansas, USA. He had registered about four thousand Indians in his club and circulated recordings of

famous musicians among its members — almost like a cassette library. Members could also buy the cassettes. The main aim of the club was to promote and propagate Indian classical music all over the world.

'Best of the Chord' was recorded at a function held at the Birla Auditorium in Jaipur. Panditji played nonstop for three hours. To facilitate a perfect acoustic effect an entire studio — microphones, speakers, recording machines, etc., were lifted from a Delhi studio and fixed at the Birla Auditorium.

Meghdootam

In 1996, the Music Today persuaded Panditji to compose melodies for the *Meghdootam* — a Sanskrit composition written by Kalidas. To Panditji it was a challenge. He toiled tirelessly for days together, consulting Sanskrit scholars, to understand the correct meanings and essence of each of the *shlokas* (verses) of *Meghdootam*. It took him time to understand, in depth, the intellectual and emotional implications of the verses.

He then set about translating them into a musical language which even a common man could understand in its totality. Panditji recalls, "This was a challenge to me. People who had done it earlier had either recited or narrated the lyrics. I composed 12 love lyrics for this album, based on different *raags* such as *Kirwani* and *Hamsadhvani*, which incidentally are also my favourite *raags*."

Top-notch singers like A. Hariharan and Kavita

Krishnamurthy lent their mellifluous voices to sing the *shlokas*. The director of Music Today coaxed Panditji into playing Mohan Veena for one of the compositions in the album, as he felt that the album would be incomplete without it. The recording was carried out at the Western Outdoor in Bombay.

The album became a rage in the Indian and international market.

The Golden Kritis of Vishwa Mohan Bhatt

In 1996 itself Panditji composed music for Pan Music — a Calcutta-based recording company. The cassette was called 'The Golden Kritis of Vishwa Mohan Bhatt'.

Here he brought about a unique fusion of north Indian and south Indian classical *raags*. The basic difference between the two streams is that the south Indian music has melodies which were written on paper by the great musicians of yesteryears like Thyagaraja, etc., and the singers just sing along these *kritis*, whereas in the north Indian classical music the scope for self-expression and self-improvization is much more. It is very difficult to merge the two musical streams, but Panditji was able to do it beautifully for the album.

With Asha Bhonsle, whose melodies he tried to play on the guitar

Sound of Strings

At the end of 1998 Music Today released 'Sound of Strings' in which Panditji played *Nat Bhairava* and *Poorvi*.

Strings of Delight

The same year he was invited to Osho Ashram to perform at the birthday celebrations of Bhagwan Rajneesh. Playing at the Buddha Auditorium, in front of a three thousand strong audience, he found the environment and ambience very inspiring. He was able to get fully immersed into the *raag* mood and depicted the emotional aspects of *raag Poorvi* with finesse. The concert was recorded live by Magnasound and released as an album entitled 'Strings of Delight' in the year 1999.

Jugalbandi with Dr. T.N. Krishnan

In 1999 itself, HMV recorded a *jugalbandi* in which Panditji combined with the veteran south Indian violin player, Dr. T.N. Krishnan. The music of the album was an amazing fusion of the north Indian musical stream and the south Indian Carnatic musical stream. It was recorded live at the prestigious Music Academy at Chennai.

Maestro of Mohan Veena

In yet another album entitled 'Maestro of Mohan Veena' he had played *raag Yaman* and *Basant,* released by Magnasound.

Raaga Varsha

In the year 2000 he recorded 'Raaga Varsha' for Dhadkan.Com, in which he played *raag Hem Bihag* and *raag Basant*.

Music for Soul

In 2001, Music Today recorded 'Music for Soul' with Pandit Bhatt.

Maestro's Choice, Kalpana

In 2004 Music Today recorded Maestro's Choice in which Panditji played *raag Maaru Bihag* and a *Pahadi dhun*. The same year a recording company called Legendary Legacy recorded 'Kalpana' in *raag Poorvi*. Panditji also recorded a rare *jugalbandi* with the vocalist Parmeshwar Hegde.

The list of his recordings is going to get longer and longer with the passage of time — each album being as melodiously enchanting as the other.

SIRIUS
ARTIST

9

The Musical Ambassador

PANDITJI'S albums recorded in his homeland had found a very good market in the West and he soon became a darling of the masses there — especially in the US and Europe. But it was only in the late 1980s that he started recording discs abroad.

Raga Records and Chhand Dhara

The first solo album which he recorded in 1988 was released under the title 'Raga Records'. In this album he played *raag Bihag*, *Desh* and *Kirwani*.

The very same year he recorded 'Chhand Dhara', released by a West Germany-based company. The album was a quintet with Daya Shankar on *shehnai*, Tarun Bhattacharya on *santoor*, Ramesh Misra on *sarangi*, Kumar Bose on *tabla* and he himself on his Mohan Veena. The album was a great success.

Facing Page: Panditji with Rock Star Narada

The Mexican guitar player David Heidalgo recorded a duet with Pandit Bhatt in 1996

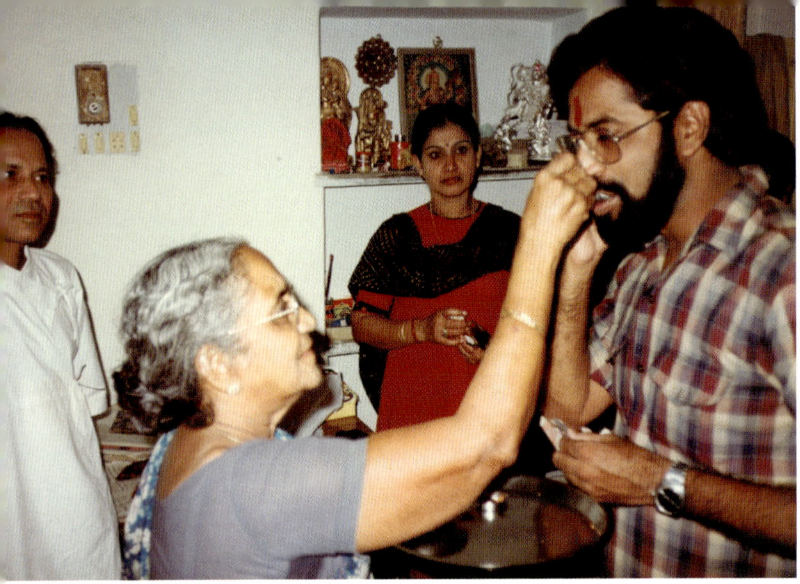

The star of her eyes — with mother Smt. Chandrakala Bhatt before departing on a foreign tour

Sardamani

Pandit Bhatt gives a lot of credit to Dr. Balwant Dixit of the University of Pittsburg (USA) for making his music popular in the West. Dr. Dixit had been playing a pivotal role in pioneering the promotion of Indian Classical music in the Western world. Dr. Dixit has organized more than two hundred concerts for Pandit Bhatt in the USA and Canada.

During one of the concerts organized by him, he introduced Panditji to Kavi Chandra Alexander — a Sri Lanka born recording engineer attached to the Waterlily Acoustics — a label specializing in audiophile quality Vinyl pressing. Mr. Alexander had been promoting high quality music from Asia and Africa with a strong emphasis on Indian classical music. This representative from the Waterlily Acoustics was so impressed with Pandit Bhatt's performance that he offered to record an album with him.

With Dr. Balwant Dixit, Mrs Dixit and Sukhwinder Singh Namdhari

Thus was recorded 'Sardamani' in which Panditji played compositions based on various Indian *raags* like *Raag Rasia* from Mathura, *Raag Maand* from Rajasthan and the *Baul* music echoing the musical strains of the fishermen of Bengal. Folk essence framed in the classical form was the basic key to the album. Pandit Bhatt was thus able to prove that folk melodies had an unconscious base in classical forms. The album was an instant hit in the market.

A Meeting by the River

Rick Turner, a legendary guitar maker from Los Angeles who had been crafting instruments for the likes of Beatles, heard the album and was so impressed by it that he requested his friend, Kavi Chandra Alexandar to play it once for Ry Cooder, an accomplished guitarist of the American Blues.

So, Mr. Alexander, sent a copy of the disc to Ry Cooder, who listened to the disc and returned it with a remark scribbled on the cover saying "The best guitar music I have ever heard. Why can't my guitar sound like this?" He also expressed a strong desire to play a *jugalbandi* (duet) with this Indian guitarist.

Pandit Bhatt was in Canada when Kavi Chandra Alexander contacted him with a request to record a *jugalbandi* with Ry Cooder. Panditji recalls, "When Kavi asked me to collaborate with Cooder, I was surprised. I neither knew Ry Cooder nor had I heard his music. I was a bit hesitant to do the duet because I am a classical musician and I like purity."

Off again! Pandit Bhatt spends more than half his time in foreign lands

Pandit Bhatt did finally accept the offer and flew down to Los Angeles to record the duet. The duet was entitled — 'A Meeting by the River'. This very meeting later brought a Grammy to the artists.

The recording of the disc was an interesting event. Ry Cooder had been recording a number for a film. After working at the studio for nearly 10 hours, he drove another two hours to meet Pandit Bhatt at his hotel in Santa Barbara. It was well past midnight when the two met for the first time in the hotel lobby. Half an hour later they were at the Christ the King's Chapel, St. Anthony's Seminary, recording their album.

While sipping tea and exchanging pleasantries and laughing they developed a dialogue in which they decided upon the course of their 'River', upon its depth and its flow. Guitars and drums were tuned and microphones positioned. The two musicians then sat down on a Persian rug near the alter and in the presence of God and the Franciscan Monks, merged their streams into a 'River' which flowed on to meet the sea of glory. The rhythm of the 'River' was provided by Sukhwinder Singh Namdhari on the *tabla* and by Ry Cooder's 14 years old son Joachim on the dumbeck.

With Sukhwinder Singh Namdhari during a recording

The sound of Pandit Bhatt's Mohan Veena contrasted and blended with the sound of Ry Cooder's bottleneck guitar. The album opened up with *raag Maand*. Later *raag Dhani*, *Nat Bhairavi* and *Tilak Kamod* flowed in.

The 'River' skirted around the *terra firma* of an ancient parable called *Mathnawi* written by the thirteenth-century Persian Sufi mystic called Jalaluddin. The parable relates the story of a frog and a mouse that meet at the riverbank to converse in a language unhindered by the rules of grammar.

The Church, in which they were recording, with its high ceiling, had a terrific acoustic quality. The late hour ensured the quiet of a studio. Recording was done on the traditional vacuum diode system without the use of any artificial amplifiers, echoes and compressors.

The architecture of the Church lent magic not only to the sound but also to the players — for there were no retakes. The recording carried on till five in the morning. By then they had recorded only 40 minutes of music. Generally a CD carries 70 minutes of music, but the artists were too tired to carry on. Panditji had to catch a flight on the same day and Ry Cooder had to return to the recording of a film music. So the two artists who had met for the first time, parted after six hours of recording — only to meet again in 1994, at the Grammy function where their composition bagged the Grammy Award.

Just after recording the album Ry Cooder is believed to have said that before Pandit Bhatt's music, his music "sounded like nursery rhymes," and that while playing he felt as if he was being "pulled by a fast horse" which was Panditji's music. This highlights the humility and greatness of Ry Cooder. Pandit Bhatt, on the other hand, calls him "an excellent Jazz guitarist."

With Simon Shaheen, The Arabian *Ud* player, with whom he recorded the album 'Sultanah'

Mr. Jayant Shah co-produced the album along with Waterlily Acoustics. Mr. Shah also played a key role in creating a wide circulation network all over USA for the album.

The album figured on the Billboard Chart for more than 40 weeks before bagging the Grammy. Billboard ratings are based on the sales figures of albums. Two other Indian musicians had figured among the Billboards top ten that year. One of them was Zakir Hussain for his 'Rhythm Experience' and the other was a singer called Sheela Chandran.

Recording a duet entitled 'Bourbon and Rosewater' with Jerry Douglas and Edgar Myre the American Dobro Guitar player

Besides the Grammy, the composition also received many other awards from different parts of the world. The Grammy Award not only catapulted Pandit Bhatt to the position of a celebrity, but also marked a turning point for Indian classical music in the West. It gave impetus to other Indian classical albums being made available overseas. The Grammy according to Panditji made him "all the more responsible." He says, "I have been playing on this Mohan Veena for so long, but after the Grammy my audiences have doubled . . . not only here in India . . . but even abroad. *Guitar Player* — an American magazine — interviewed me. *Folk Roots* a magazine of U.K., put me on their cover. But what makes me happy is that I am reaching audiences of all ages and regions."

Some people suffer from the wrong notion that by going in for fusion music, Panditji had gone against tradition. Panditji counters saying, "Classical music is my life. The new-age world music fusions in which I have forayed, comprised a different form of my musical expression. For me fusion music is entirely a new region of musical expression in which I emulate the classical form in a very dexterous and skilled manner. This is a completely different stream which in no way damages or tampers with the sanctity of classical music."

Pandit Bhatt was, however, not the first to start experimenting with fusion music. The trend was set by Pandit Ravi Shankar and the ace violinist Yehudi Menuhin in 1967, when they recorded 'West meets East' — a *jugalbandi* which won the maestros a special Grammy.

It is sad that the disc of 'A Meeting by the River' was not made available in India. Kavi Chandra Alexander did send some copies to India, which were sold by a Bombay music shop at an exorbitant price. The price had to be hiked to cover the steep duties levied by the Government on discs recorded abroad.

Before 'A Meeting by the River', Waterlily Acoustics was a very small label with a very narrow reach, but after the Grammy it became a world-renowned company. This company has recorded most of Panditji's discs released abroad.

With Sukhwinder Singh Namdhari
who provided the rhythm to "A Meeting by the River"

Explorations

After this magnanimous fusion of the Indian and American music, Panditji recorded an album called 'Explorations' with a company called Mantra Music of New York. In this he played *raga Bhairavi* and *Desh*. The disc was released in 1995.

Music takes him beyond the temporal, to a level from where he communicates with the cosmic composers

Gathering Rain Clouds

In 1995 itself, the Waterlily Acoustics recorded 'Gathering Rain Clouds'. In this album Panditji played *Miya Malhar* and *Gavati*. The romance of thunder and pouring rain has been depicted so beautifully in the album, that one can almost smell the nostalgic fragrance of the freshly drenched earth. In India, *Miya Malhar* is considered to be a magical *raag*. It is believed that when Tansen (the great musician of Akbar's Court) and his daughter sang *Malhar*, the rain gods used to be so pleased that they sent down heavy rain. Once Tansen was singing *Raag Deepak* (lamp). As he went deep into the *raag* his body began to burn. Fearing that her father might perish, his daughter then started singing *Malhar*. The Rain Gods obliged and sent down pouring rain, which put out the fire on Tansen's body. After that incident Tansen never sang *raag Deepak* again.

Something similar happened in Chandigarh in 1997. When Panditji started playing *Malhar* in front of a large audience — the heavens started pouring rain. Whether it was a co-incidence or the magic of Mohan Veena — one cannot say — but the incident will remain etched in the minds of his listeners forever.

Mumtaz Mahal

In 1995 Panditji recorded another fusion with an American music singer who had named himself Taj Mahal. Their album was aptly called 'Mumtaz Mahal' (the empress in whose memory emperor Shahjahan had constructed the monument of Taj Mahal). Waterlily Acoustics recorded the album at the very same Church

'V' is for Vishwa Mohan, says Carlos Santana,
while Pandit Bhatt beams

Legends all — Pt. Bhatt, John McLaughlin and Jeff Beck

"Your music touches my heart", says John McLaughlin to Pandit Bhatt

With Ustad Zakir Hussain

With rock star Steve Y in Dallas

That was hilarious — sharing a joke with a friend

Flanked by beautiful admirers

Pt. Bhatt affectionately puts an arm around Eric Clapton's shoulder

How are my albums doing in the market?
— Pt. Bhatt

With George Harrison
who is an admirer of Pt. Bhatt's music

in Santa Barbara, where other fusion albums were recorded. According to Panditji the choice of the venue was not due to any superstition but because of a "sound ear for sound reasons." The album, which is very melodious ends with a sort of musical dialogue between the two artists in which they seem to be planning a number, they might play in future. Panditji hums a tune and the album ends abruptly — leaving the listener yearning for more.

Bourbon and Rosewater

In 1996 came 'Bourbon and Rosewater' — also released by the Waterlily Acoustics — in which Panditji played a *jugalbandi* with the American Dobro Guitar player Jerry Douglas. A Dobro guitar is an old 1920s model of a guitar. It has a very deep and rich sound, which can well be compared to the sound of the Mohan Veena in its richness, sweep, slide and clarity.

Jerry Douglas had listened to 'A Meeting by the River' several times and had become an ardent admirer of Pandit Vishwa Mohan Bhatt. In his heart he cherished a desire to play a *jugalbandi* with Panditji. So when in 1995 he was sponsored by the American Embassy to play in India, he expressed a desire to play at Jaipur, Panditji's hometown. As soon as he landed at the Jaipur airport he wanted to meet Pandit Bhatt. Unfortunately, Panditji was out of town.

Pt. Bhatt however returned, just in time to listen to Jerry Douglas' performance at the Jawahar Kala Kendra. After the performance Jerry Douglas invited Pandit Bhatt and his son Salil

Bhatt for dinner at the Rajputana Sheraton Hotel, where he again expressed his desire to play a duet with Panditji.

Panditji had also loved the way Jerry Douglas played his Dobro Guitar. So the two decided that someday they would play together.

In 1996 when Panditji visited USA, he contacted Jerry Douglas and 'Bourbon and Rosewater' was recorded at the dead of night in Christ the King's Chapel in Santa Barbara and released by the Waterlily Acoustics the same year.

In the album both the artists have just let out their hearts. More than 90 per cent of it was improvized during the recording. It, indeed, was a uniquely delectable blend of the Eastern and Western musical outpourings. After listening to the album George Harrison is believed to have commented "an exceptional recording by my favourite musician."

Tabula Rasa

In 1996 itself, the Waterlily Acoustics recorded another fusion in which Panditji combined with an American Banjo player, Bela Fleck and a Chinese artist Jie Beng Chen on her Erhu. The Erhu is a two stringed instrument played like the violin with a bow. The album was named 'Tabula Rasa', which literally means 'a clean slate' — for here was a music with a distinct flavour, the kind which had never existed before. The album was recorded at night in a matter of just seven hours, without the use of any artificial sound effects.

With George Harrison and his wife

In Canada with Padma

It was presented in four parts. It started as a *jugalbandi* followed by vigorous solo sequences, *in tandem*, creating a dizzying effect. The intrinsic emotion conveyed in the album was that of elation through discovery, hedged by suspense. Its soothing yet invigorating appeal sold very well in the American music market.

According to Panditji, Bela Fleck, Jie Beng Chen and he himself had given their best and finest parts to the music of this album. It was nominated for the Grammy in 1997 — but history did not repeat itself.

Pandit Bhatt was the first artist in thousands of years of Indo-Chinese history to have created a *jugalbandi* with a renowned Chinese artist. According to Panditji, it was her delightful folk music, which inspired him to record an album with her.

Silk Jade and the Begging Bowl

He recorded another album with Jie Beng Chen called 'Silk Jade and the Begging Bowl' It was also released by the Waterlily Acoustics. Panditji explains, "The Chinese music system has mostly pentatonic melodies — much like our Indian *raags Durga*, *Sarang* and *Bhopali*. A particular melody that Jie Beng Chen played was close to our *raag Bhopali*, the *hyam* onwards. So I played the Chinese melody as the *asthayee* and she played the *murchhana* on her instrument . . . with each stroke on our instruments we looked into each other's eyes and it was as if we knew what the other was saying. It was an unforgettable experience."

The compositions were based on an eight beat rhythm cycle. No percussion instruments were used. The music was a wholehearted communion without words — and it spoke volumes. What better mode could there have been of extending the hand of friendship to India's Chinese neighbour.

Sultanah

Pandit Bhatt had the distinction of being the first Indian artist to record an album with an Arabian artist — thus giving a new dimension to Indo-Arab relations. Pandit Bhatt teamed up with Simon Shaheen; the New York based Arab Musician who played the *Ud* — a rare Arabian instrument, considered to be an ancient form of the Indian *sarod*. *Ud* is also very similar to the *lute* and the *rabab*. It has been played in the Arabian deserts since pre-Islamic times. The album was called the 'Sultanah.'

This Indo-Arab *jugalbandi* was admittedly Shaheen's idea. He had been listening to Pandit Bhatt's music and had developed a fascination for it. So he approached Panditji with the concept of an East meets Middle East fusion, when the two met after Pandit Bhatt's performance at the Mahatma Gandhi's 125th birth anniversary celebrations at Lincoln centre in New York. Panditji also liked the idea of playing together.

So the two artists set about synchronizing the Mohan Veena with the Arabian *Ud*. The recording was performed at midnight in the very same chapel at Santa Barbara, by the very same recording company — Waterlily Acoustics.

All the compositions on the disc were based on Indian *raags*, which included *Kirwani*, *Bhopali*, *Dhani* and *Chandrakauns*. One of the compositions was based on *raga Piloo*, which Pandit Bhatt, rendered so beautifully, with all its grandeur and romance. Panditji recalls, "as we sat down to set the compositions, 90 per cent of it came through improvization."

The scintillating duets echoed the undulating sand dunes and the cold and lonely nights of the desert. According to Panditji this was one of his best fusions. It really conquered the hearts of both the Indian and Arabian music lovers.

Panditji also discovered that there was a great similarity between the Arabian *makam*s (musical scales) and Indian *ragas*, especially those of Carnatic music. The Arabs use micro tones or what Indians call *shruti*s, occurring in between the *svar*s. In India this feature is found in folk music of some regions like Bengal and Rajasthan. Panditji also discovered that Arabian musicians use equivalents of Indian aesthetic graces such as *gamaks*, *meend*, *taan*, and *andolan*s.

The album was not just a harmonious blend of two completely different cultural and musical streams but was also a meeting of the old and the new. The musical notes from Pandit Bhatt's new Mohan Veena blended so beautifully with the music from Simon Shaheen's ancient *Ud*.

The two artists later performed together in Israel and at the Merkin Concert Hall in New York.

Fusion Music with David Heidalgo

Late in 1996, Waterlily Acoustics recorded another album in which Panditji played with the Mexican guitar player David Heidalgo. Panditji's son Salil Bhatt also accompanied the two artists in the album. The music was based mainly on Mexican folk tunes with a great emphasis on the rhythm — provided by the Indian percussion instrument *mridangam*.

This was the very first time Salil Bhatt was playing a fusion with a foreign artist — but he was able to manoeuvre through it with finesse.

Kavi Chandra Alexander was very impressed by Salil's performance that day so he offered to record a duet of the father and son, on the following day. It was again during the quiet of the night that Salil on his Mohan Veena recorded a duet with his genius father. They played *raags Bihag*, *Bhopali* and *Kirwani*.

Indian Delta & Swar Shikhar

In 2002, Sense World an English recording company, recorded 'Indian Delta'. In this album Pandit Bhatt played the *raags Puria Dhanashri* and *Shyam Kalyan*. In 2002 itself, Virgin Records, recorded 'Swar Shikhar' in which Panditji played a *jugalbandi* with his son Salil. They played *raag Jog*.

Mohan Veena

In 2003 Sense World Music again recorded another *jugalbandi* with the father and son called 'Mohan Veena', in which they played *raags Bageshwari*, *Tilak Kamod* and a dhun in *Maand*.

Speaking about his fusions recorded with foreign artists Panditji observes, "I have found that these spirited ventures have enriched me as a musician. Having opened my mind to experiment with all these world music streams, I have opened up new horizons for Indian classical music, where it can develop further and henceforth bring out some unique intricacies. I have tried to redefine classical music for the next millennium."

♪ 10 ♪

Raag-Ragini

MUSIC is the language of the heart, flowing out from its depths in melodious currents while washing away its woes and providing succour to its joys. Music expressed through Indian classical *raags* encompasses a very wide range of emotional patterns. According to Panditji, "The Indian system of *raags* has such a wide range, depth and scope that we do not need to create new *raags*." He believes, "there are so many *raags* which many artists do not even know of. There are *raags* such as *Tanki* and *Jungla*, which very few have heard of. So there is need for much research."

Each *raag* has its own emotional colour and mood, its own pace and beauty. Even though Panditji loves all *raags*, there are a few *raags*, which he is very fond of. It is a fact, that an artist can express his imagination and emotions with more precision, ease and lucidity, if he uses his favourite *raags*.

Concord

Panditji loves *raag Yaman*. The *raag* expresses the mood of *bhakti* — gentle, pious and pure. According to him the *raag* "takes you above the temporal, to a level from where you can have a direct communion with God." Panditji feels that *raag Yaman* has a strange spiritual quality. "When you use the *shuddha gandhar* in the *raag*, it brings out a feeling of peace, contentment and joy. You feel relaxed," he holds. He believes that "when a man is tired or irritated and he hears *raag Yaman* — its *alap* in *vilambit laya*, its *gandhar* and *nishad svars* (notes) . . . and when *shadaj* is introduced — the individual forgets his problems and experiences a strange peace."

According to Panditji there are other serious *raags* like *Kausi Kanhra*, *Darbari*, *Poorvi*, *Bageshwari* and *Rageshwari*, which he loves to play. To him these *raags* depict a mood of undisturbed earnestness and resolute concentration. Essentially these *raags* convey deep and serious sentiments. Panditji uses these melodies to ease his tensions and to express the beauty of pain.

Posing with his instrument

Panditji strongly believes in the celebration of life. He wants to spend each moment of his life with enthusiasm, joy and happiness — and wants others to do the same. He believes that life is a precious gift from God. He, therefore, loves *raag Bihag* — *Maru Bihag* and *Hem Bihag*. "These *raags* besides possessing the qualities of *raag Yaman*, convey a mood of festivity and celebration. They enthuse one with a happy mood," he holds.

Another *raag* that Panditji often uses to express the mood of celebration and jubilation is *raag Hamsadhvani*. He recalls

"When I composed 'Music for Relaxation' I based it on *raag Hamsadhvani*. The *raag* depicts a festive mood like that of Deepawali, when everything around is bright and vibrant. After creating the composition I met a lot of people and asked them what kind of images the composition evoked in their minds. They said they visualized images of sparkling festivity."

Panditji believes that each *raag* has its own pace. "Some *raags* move at the pace of an elephant while others run at the pace of a deer. While playing a particular *raag* one has to keep in mind its intrinsic pace. You cannot use an elephant pace *raag* and make it run like a deer. You have to abide by the *raag dharma* while playing it," he says.

11

Memorable Performances

PANDIT Bhatt stepped on foreign land for the first time in the late 1970s, when he visited USA. Since then he has been performing extensively in Canada, Britain, Wales, Scotland, USA, Switzerland, France, Belgium, Germany, Netherlands, Australia, Ireland, Singapore, Russia and the Gulf countries. He is also a visiting Professor to 16 universities in the United States of America. The 150 odd stickers on his "Mohan Veena" case bear evidence to the fact that he spends more than half of his time abroad.

Pandit Bhatt has in fact played a major role in popularizing Indian classical music in the West. According to Panditji, "the appeal of Indian classical music lies in its spiritual nature, in its ability to encompass all human emotions and inspirations." He believes that, "the West has now come to realize that Indian musical heritage is rich enough to encompass all musical shades discovered elsewhere so far." Panditji's tours to foreign lands have also helped him in understanding the nuances of Western music.

Performance at Belfast

He was the first Indian musician to perform in Belfast, the capital of the trouble-torn Northern Ireland. In fact, his concert was the main attraction at the week long Belfast Festival held at the famous Empire Music Hall. The concert was organized by the Asian Music Circuit — a London-based institute, working for the promotion of Indian music. Ireland was at that time a country where the rich musical and cultural heritage of India was relatively unknown. Panditji played his "Mohan Veena" with such distinction that he mesmerized the Irish audience. He was accompanied by his son Salil. At the end of the performance the audience was so enthralled that they gave the artists a standing ovation. Pandit Bhatt felt that the honour received in Belfast was not merely for himself but for his country as well.

With Anuradha Paudwal

Performance to Commemorate 100 years of BBC

Panditji gave solo concerts at the Royal Albert Hall in August 1994 to commemorate 100 years of BBC and at the Lincoln Institute in

New York as a part of the Concerts for Peace, marking the 125th birth anniversary celebrations of Mahatma Gandhi.

Rag Ganga at the Golden Jubilee Celebrations of India's Independence in London

Another memorable performance that Pandit Bhatt gave was at the Royal Albert Hall in London on 10th July, 1997. The concert marked the beginning of the Golden Jubilee Celebrations of India's Independence. Prince Charles was the Chief Guest at the function. The 50th year of India's Independence had stirred up the feelings of every Indian. Each one responded to the occasion in his own way. The Grammy Award winner expressed his feelings through *Raag Ganga* — his new creation that led the listeners through the freedom struggle to the post-Independence era in India.

The Indians consider River Ganga to be a holy river. A number of tributaries join in during its course. Pandit Bhatt's *Raag Ganga* was a confluence of various Indian classical *raags*, which lost their identity as they merged together to form the new *raag*. Just as the Ganga flows tirelessly over a vast and varied terrain, *Raag Ganga* took listeners along the long and varied phases of the pre and post-Independence India.

The first part of the *raag* signified the pre-Independence rebellion. It expressed the condition of the freedom-fighters who wanted to attain freedom at any cost. The composition created a picture of pain and agony of those who were imprisoned and

With Ustad Allah Rakha and Zakir Hussain

tortured — only because they wanted to be free. Here Panditji chiefly used *raag Charukeshi* with *raags Todi* and *Bhatiyar* merging in.

The second part in the *raag* expressed the ecstatic jubilation at the midnight of 14th August, 1947 when India awoke to a dawn of freedom. The feeling of pain disappeared as *raag hamsadhwani* put the listeners in a cheerful mood.

The third and the final part of *Raag Ganga* depicted the post-Independence period in Indian history. It began on a serious note expressing gratitude to those who had lost their lives during the freedom struggle. The serious melody with its slow and steady rhythm also denoted the onerous task of nation-building.

Gradually the music quickened its pace. The rhythm denoted progress made in the different fields of national life. It denoted the desire of the youth to change the face of the nation. Pandit Bhatt harnessed *raags Jog* and *Bihag* to express these emotions.

The treachery of the German Winter

Panditji always wears an exotic silk *kurta* and *churidar payjama* for all his performances — even in extremely cold conditions. This rigidity to the dressing code sometimes creates problems for him.

Once he was to give a recital at a place in Germany during the height of winter. It was snowing heavily all around. Panditji, wearing his *kurta-payjama* and *chappal*s (slippers) sat snugly, enjoying the warmth of the car, which was carrying him to the auditorium. He was quite sure that he would have to take just one step into the cold before getting inside the comfortably heated auditorium. But things went a little awry that day. The snow outside was too thick to allow his car to reach the auditorium gates and he had to step down on to the piercingly cold snow. At each step his feet sank into the biting snow. The short distance to the gate seemed miles long. At last when he reached the auditorium his feet had become totally numb and felt like wood. His hands, which move on the Mohan Veena, like lightning, were also frozen stiff and he wondered how he would perform on stage that day.

There were still two hours left for the performance. He said a little prayer, immediately borrowed an overcoat to warm himself, and somehow managed to warm his frozen hands and feet. By God's grace the magic returned to his hands and the concert was a great success.

Fun at the Bowling Alley in Philadelphia

Something equally awful happened when he was to perform at a concert in Philadelphia. He and his *tabla* player, Sukhwinder Singh Namdhari had reached the city two days in advance. So the organizer of the concert decided to entertain them during this period, by taking them around the city. On the morning of the concert day, he came up with the bright idea of taking the artists to a bowling alley.

At the alley, the three of them were having such a great time that they totally forgot that they had a concert lined up for the evening. Suddenly, to their dismay, they realized that the very two fingers and thumb, which they use to play their respective

The biting snow has numbed my feet

Let us change the attire

With Ustad Ali Akbar Khan

instruments, were becoming stiff, tired and painful. They looked at each other and wondered what had come upon them to take such a risk and immediately wound up their game.

By the time they reached their hotel, the pain and stiffness in their hands had increased. The artists were really very worried now. They desperately tried out some hand exercises to flex the joints. Gradually, after a lot of effort, the stiffness and pain began to ease, and by evening the pain and stiffness had disappeared totally. But a little fear still lingered on in their hearts, that something might just go wrong with the movement of their fingers during the concert.

They went up on stage praying to Goddess Sarasvati to work some kind of magic on them — and the magic did work. The concert was an unbelievable success.

Rajasthan Divas

Rajasthan Divas (Day) is celebrated every year in Jaipur, on 30th March. In 1998 the Rajasthan Government invited Pandit Bhatt to perform at the celebrations. Panditji agreed to perform, but wanted to be accompanied by a team of local instrumentalists. Rajasthan has a variety of interesting folk instruments whose distant strains have not reached most people living in cities. The plight of these folk artists brought to Panditji's mind the touching lines by Thomas Gray, which said,

> Full many a flower is born to blush unseen,
> and waste its sweetness on the desert air.

The talents of these folk instrumentalists had blossomed in the lonely distant deserts of Rajasthan. By and large, the city people had not been able to derive pleasure from the sweetness that their music showered upon the auditory sensibilities. Panditji felt that there could not be a better time than the Rajasthan Divas to bring these folk artists out into the limelight. So he decided to lead an ethnic orchestra which included a variety of folk instruments.

One of the instruments he chose was the Sindhi *sarangi* whose sombre tones could touch the deepest depths of pathos. The instrument was originally brought to India from Sindh in Pakistan. It is now being manufactured in the Falaudi area of Rajasthan.

The sound of flute in the orchestra coloured the melody with shades of nostalgia.

Khartal, which is nothing but a set of four pieces of flat wood, was played by Kohinoor Langa from Barmer. The real name of Kohinoor Langa is Bundu Khan. Bundu had once played the *khartal* in front of Queen Elizabeth in London. He was barely eight years old then. Thrilled by his performance the queen had called him the 'Kohinoor of India'. Since then Bundu Khan prefers to call himself Kohinoor Langa. It is fascinating to hear the variety of permutations and combinations of rhythm, which these four pieces of wood can create in a pair of magical hands.

With Pandit Shiv Kumar Sharma, Ustad Zakir Hussain and his wife

An instrument that caught the interest of the public most was *Bhapang*. Played by the muslim *jogis* of northern Rajasthan, it had derived its form from the *Damaroo* of Lord Shiva. Unlike the *Damaroo* it had skin at one end only — the other end remained uncovered. A string attached to the skin flowed out of the hollow. The artist held the instrument under the left arm and pulled the string with the left hand while striking the string with the right hand — thus creating sounds which suggested the gurgling notes of a rivulet.

With the royal family of Jaipur and Asha Bhonsle

To top it all, the powerful clarity of musical notes gushing out of the Mohan Veena, seemed to stir up the entire cosmos. Percussion instruments such as *pakhawaj* and *dholak* provided pace to the graceful flow of melody, thereby highlighting its beauty.

Watching Panditji rehearse with these humble folk artists was quite an experience. The atmosphere during the practice sessions was always relaxed and happy. Panditji displayed respect for each artist and his talent. He valued their suggestions and made each one feel important. The team spirit enthused in the group was a fine example of an efficient leadership. The program was also a roaring success.

Performance at the Indo-Pak Summit on 15th July, 2001

A performance that will remain the most memorable for Panditji was the one when he had to perform for the Indo-Pak Summit at Agra on 15th July, 2001.

The world had set its eyes on the Summit. People hoped that peace, calm and brotherhood would descend upon the relations between the two countries.

For Panditji it was a great honour to be invited to perform before the esteemed guests and dignitaries. In fact, he was the only musician who was invited to perform for the occasion.

He was given a week's time to prepare. Even before he could give it a thought, his house was flooded with media personnel. Press and camera teams started hounding him for comments on what he would play and what would be his message through the musical language.

Agra, for that occasion, was full of dignitaries, security staff and thousands of members of the press, from all over the world. Panditji, along with his family, reached Agra a day ahead of the concert. He was to be assisted on stage by his two sons, his wife and his daughter-in-law.

They were made to stay at the Oberoi Hotel. Inspite of all the comfort, they could not sleep at night — feelings of anticipation and excitement being too strong to allow them to sleep peacefully. The family fully realized the responsibility which lay upon their shoulders. They felt they were there to represent the Indian musical tradition and to display its beauty to the honoured guests. They were there to evoke feelings of *sadbhavana* (amity)

Sailing smoothly

among the participants. The piece that Panditji had specially composed for the occasion was also named *Sadbhavana*, based on *raag Bihag*.

The next morning even before Panditji could take his breakfast, a team from Zee-TV hijacked him to their makeshift studio at the Mughal Sheraton. The team wanted their channel to be the first to telecast an interview with Panditji.

This interview was followed by another six hours of interviews by press teams from different parts of the world. There was no time for him to even take a bite for lunch. By the end of it all, he was so tired that he just wanted to flee from scene. He

Even Mrs. Sonia Gandhi loves his music

needed to take a little rest before the concert at the JP Palace Hotel later in the evening.

At the JP Palace Hotel security was extremely tight. The family was checked three times by the security staff. Then they were led into the huge banquet hall decorated with a profusion of the most beautiful varieties of flowers one could ever see. The hotel staff took no time in getting the stage ready as per Panditji's requirements.

With President Musharraf, Begum Musharraf, (former) Prime Minister Atal Behari Vajpayee, ministers, politicians, dignitaries and other guests seated in front, Panditji began the concert by hoping and wishing that love, peace, amity and brotherhood would descend upon the relations between the two countries.

He played for half an hour, accompanied by his two sons on their respective Mohan Veenas and his wife and daughter-in-law on the *tanapuras*. One could see total involvement and concentration on Panditji's face while he played, for this was an occasion being watched by the entire world. Panditji really gave his best that day.

President Parvez Musharraf was listening to him with rapt attention. For the entire half an hour nothing moved in the hall except the fingers of the artists.

At the end, they got a standing ovation from the audience.

During the dinner that followed Panditji presented a CD of his album 'The Lure of the Desert' to President Musharraf. The

"I have made your India proud" at Madame Tussauds, London — posing in front of the wax figures of Mahatma Gandhi and Smt. Indira Gandhi

With Sukanya Ravi Shankar

"I admire them both" — with V.G. Jog and Srimati Chandra Kala Bhatt

President said, he would love to hear it in the mornings. He was very appreciative of Panditji's performance. He had liked the deep and vibrant sound of the Mohan Veena. Begum Musharraf was also very impressed and said to him, "*aisa lagta hai ki apke upar Allah ka fazal hai. apke hathon me kuchh jadu hai* (I feel you have God's blessings on you. There is magic in your hands)."

(Former) Prime Minister Atal Behari Vajpayee hugged Panditji and told him that he had shown the world how beautiful Indian classical music was.

That day's performance proved the fact that music has no political boundaries. It only connects hearts by forming bridges of love.

In tune with the Langas and Manganiars — the folk instrumentalists of Rajasthan

♪ 12 ♪

From the Eyes of Sandip Das The Tabla Player

IT is the *tabla* which provides pulse and pace to melody. Sandip Das — bracketed among the top *tabla* players of India — has been accompanying Panditji on his concert tours ever since 1988. Hailing from Patna, he is one of the favourite disciples of Pandit Kishan Maharaj, the doyen of the Banaras *gharana*.

As Sandip Das plays, his hand just sweeps down like a gust of wind on the skin of the *tabla*, breaking into an explosive, rapid rumble. He knows just when and how to add his own touches to a recital and when to keep a low profile. On the whole, Sandip Das gives perfect accompaniment to Pandit Bhatt's recitals.

Having worked closely with Panditji for so many years, he has many interesting incidents to relate, which throw light upon the character and personality of the maestro.

According to Sandip Das, Panditji is very apt at assessing the mood of the

With Shri Sandip Das, the *tabla* player who provides pulse and pace to his music

audience. He generally selects the piece he should play, after taking into account the type of audience present and their mood. This is the reason why all his concerts are successful. "You make him sit with connoisseurs of classical music and he will excel and play accordingly and you make him sit with school students who do not understand classical music and he comes out with flying colours," says Sandip Das.

Way back in 1988, when Sandip Das was still studying at Patna University, a concert had been organized in which some of the top ranking classical artists were to perform in front of the students. Sandip Das had made great efforts to get Panditji to play for this concert. Unfortunately, the audience that day was in no mood to listen to classical music. The noisy atmosphere in the concert hall was so bad that many of the artists decided not to play at all. But Panditji was undeterred, for he knew that he could handle the situation.

Autograph seekers

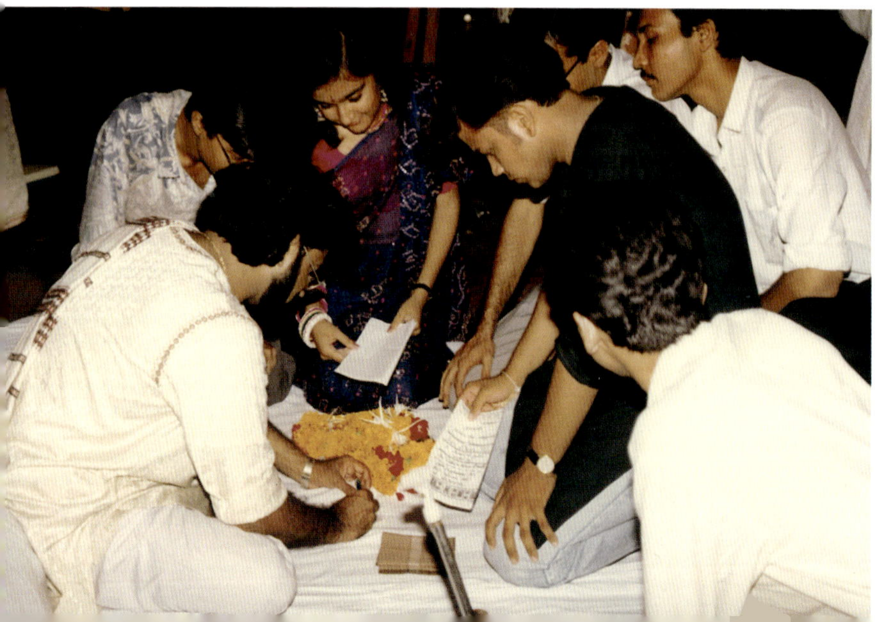

Before beginning his recital he took the microphone and addressed the gathering saying, "I know you are in a mood to make a noise and have fun. If I was your age I too would have loved to do the same," and soon he was able to build a rapport with the youngsters and calm them down. The students were now ready to listen to an artist who felt and thought like them. He continued saying, "You youngsters are under a false notion

Building a rapport with the audience
before beginning a recital

that classical music is slow and dull. Just listen to my music and at the end do let me know if you were right or wrong." With this challenge he began his recital. The students really relished the performance and at the end gave a thunderous applause. "Thus he changed the evening, which was doomed for disaster, into a success," says Sandip Das.

Sandip Das respects Panditji for many reasons. "For one, Panditji is very serious about his sound. There are many artists who reach the auditorium just in time for the performance. Once on stage they start giving all kinds of signals to people at the controls. In fact, they don't really care much about the sound that people are getting. Pandit Vishwa Mohan makes it a point to reach the auditorium well in advance — generally two hours ahead. He goes on stage along with his accompanists to do all the sound checks and balancing and is back again in the wings at least 15 minutes before the performance. He never takes even a small concert less seriously. To him every concert is important. This is one of the reasons why he is there at the top," feels Sandip Das.

Sandip Das admires him for his efforts at popularizing classical music in India as well as abroad. Pandit Bhatt is doing a lot of concerts for Spic Macay — an organization involved in the task of promoting classical music amongst the youth. Panditji charges nothing for these concerts. There are many other organizations for which Panditji plays voluntarily with not the least concern for money — and he does at least two such concerts every month.

Sandip Das will never forget one such Spic Macay concert organized at a school in Nainital. The school was located at the top of a very steep hill. The winding road leading to it was extremely narrow. As the jeep carrying Panditji and Sandip Das roared up the precariously steep motor way, the artists were gripped by an awful vertiginous dread. Each moment, they feared they would tumble down into the deep valley. The best of assurances by the expert driver could not dry out the cold sweat, that broke out on the two apprehensive artists.

After a Spic Macay Concert at the Delhi Public School

Suddenly a car coming down the hill blocked their way up. All that their driver could do was to start reversing till he could find a wide enough patch for the other car to pass by. Sandip Das, totally unwilling to risk his life, decided to step out of the car, but Panditji felt that he had to help the driver. He would rather take a plunge down the hill than leave the poor driver to take the risk alone! So he sat through the awesome backslide, praying all the time. When finally they reached the peak, they thanked God for having carried them up this dangerous climb, safely. The concert too was a great success. This was a concert, which will always remain etched on the minds of the artists.

Sandip Das remembers a number of concerts when the audience would just not let them go. The organizers and the auditorium staff would want them to pack up, but the people would just not let them get off the stage.

According to Sandip Das, Panditji can be a bit too polite, at times. Once the two were invited to perform at a concert in Aligarh. The arrangements made for the artists by the organizers were very deplorable. Panditji kept complaining to Sandip Das about the poor arrangements. Sandip Das, who was himself very unhappy about it all, got carried away by Panditji's complaints and just walked up to the organizers and gave them hell for having made Panditji so uncomfortable. The organizers were sorry for it all, and decided to apologize to Panditji. Faced by the organizers, "Panditji was now all kindness, forgiveness and forbearance personified," recalls Sandip. He kept telling the organizers, "Oh, such things happen at times. It doesn't matter. Do not worry. It's alright. . . ." The organizers who all this while had been thinking that Panditji was furious, now turned to Sandip Das and gave him a look which said, "here is a great artist who is humane enough to forgive us, and there you are, a youngster, making all this noise." That day Sandip Das decided never to get provoked by Panditji's complaints.

"Panditji is unbelievably polite even with his students. To them, he is more of a friend than a *guru*. A *shishya* will never hesitate to ring him up, just to make him repeat a *taan* he has forgotten. Most *gurus* would instead fire the student for having forgotten it. In fact, students would never take such a liberty with any other *guru* — but Panditji is a fellow human first and then a *guru*," observes Sandip Das.

Panditji is very fond of narrating jokes. All you have to do is to, somehow, put him in that mood. So he can be a very good companion, especially while travelling.

The quality of a *tabla* player's performance depends to a great extent on the artist he is playing with. If put with a very good artist the *tabla* player's level of performance also rises. Sandip Das is grateful to Panditji for having helped him improve.

Happiness — with son Saurabh

13

Panditji and God

More things are wrought by prayer than this world dreams of.

— Tennyson

PANDIT Vishwa Mohan is a person who whole-heartedly believes in these words. To him God is a living presence. He strongly believes that there is God's inspiration in everyone's life; the important thing is to discover it and converse with that divine force. He says, "I believe in God, but differently. Not by getting up at the crack of dawn to do *puja*! I think that God has to be felt inside. It may be *Kalyug* but the heart is still the domain of God. The devil can invade only till the mind. You must listen to your inner voice. It will always tell you the right thing." To Panditji classical music is the medium which takes him beyond worldly affairs, away from excitement, towards soothing of the spirits.

He experiences certain divine vibrations when he

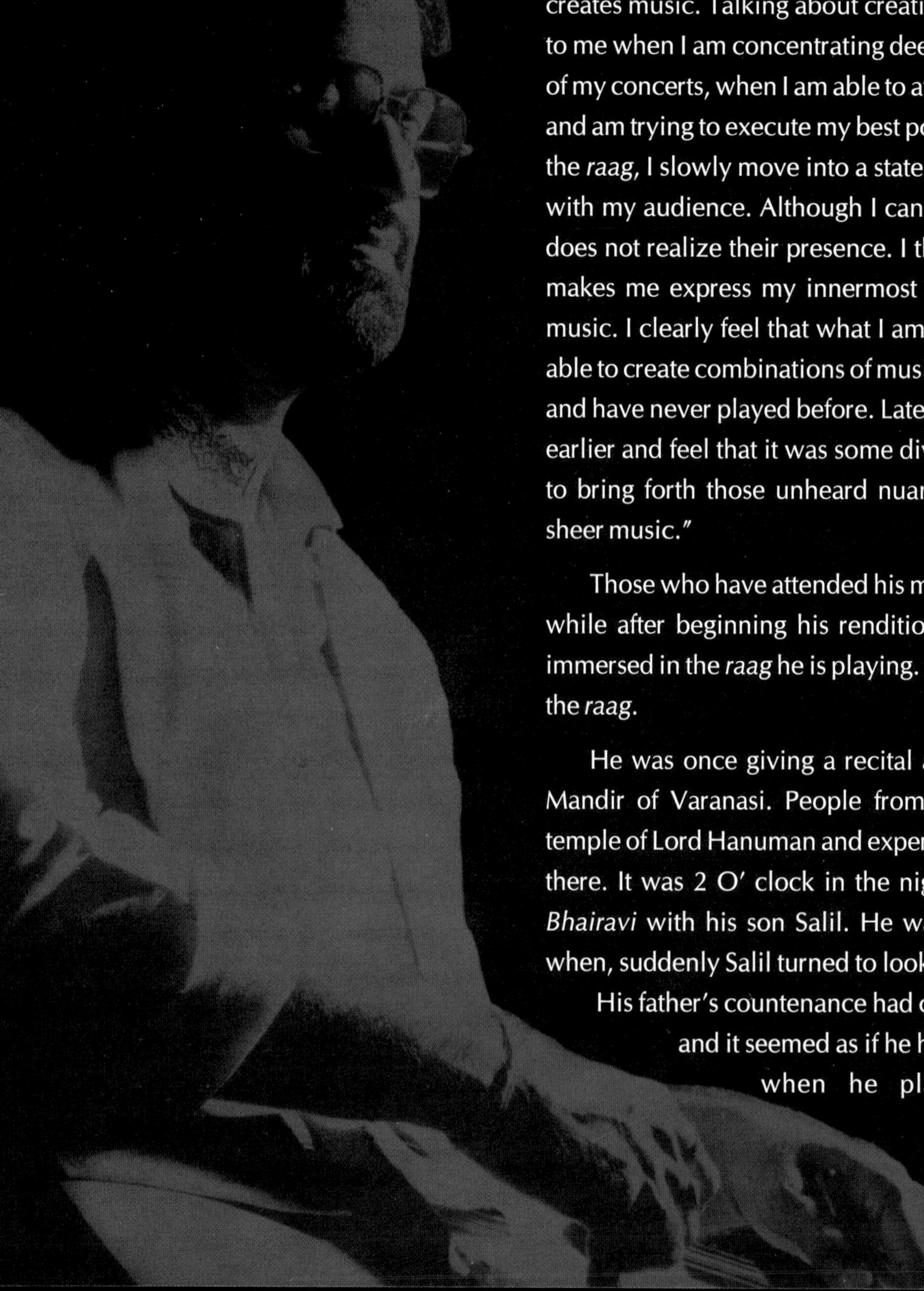

creates music. Talking about creativity he says, "Creativity comes to me when I am concentrating deeply in my music. During some of my concerts, when I am able to attain a perfect vision of my *raag* and am trying to execute my best possible imagination to enhance the *raag*, I slowly move into a state of trance, where I lose contact with my audience. Although I can see them, my mind and body does not realize their presence. I then experience a force, which makes me express my innermost thoughts of devotion through music. I clearly feel that what I am rendering is beyond me. I am able to create combinations of musical notes, which I do not know and have never played before. Later, I marvel at what I had played earlier and feel that it was some divine power which enabled me to bring forth those unheard nuances and intricate passages of sheer music."

Those who have attended his music concerts know that a little while after beginning his renditions he gets totally and deeply immersed in the *raag* he is playing. He virtually becomes one with the *raag*.

He was once giving a recital at the famous Sankat Mochan Mandir of Varanasi. People from all over the world visit this temple of Lord Hanuman and experience certain divine vibrations there. It was 2 O' clock in the night. Panditji was playing *raag Bhairavi* with his son Salil. He was deep into playing the *raag* when, suddenly Salil turned to look at his father and was stunned. His father's countenance had changed. His face was glowing and it seemed as if he had gone into a trance. Usually when he plays, he looks around at his accompanists, smiles at them, expresses appreciation and encourages them. But right now he was totally unaware of himself and of the thousands of people who surrounded him. It seemed as if divinity was flowing into him from above. As the *raag* mounted to the *jhala* stage it became evident that he had been totally filled up with a divine presence. The audience also sat absolutely still with their eyes fixed on Panditji's face and their hearts and minds hooked on to his rendition.

Salil began to feel that the divine vibrations after overflowing his father, were now touching him from time to time. The *tabla* player Vikram Ghosh also felt the same way.

There was a thunderous applause from the audience at the end of the concert. They were shouting "Jai Hanuman" and "Har Har Mahadev." When Panditji came down from the stage they just picked him up over their heads. They felt they had seen Goddess Sarasvati in Panditji and were, therefore, overwhelmed with the experience.

A recordist had been assigned the task of recording the programme. He had switched on the recording system at the beginning of the concert — but to everyone's surprise not a sound had been recorded. It was God's will! The recordist was totally amazed by this occurrence.

On the whole, it was an unforgettable experience for those present. Panditji took nearly 10 minutes to come back to his original form. It was only then that he started recognizing people and responding to them.

Recalling the incident, Panditji says that at that time he felt as if he was playing effortlessly. A divine force was telling him what to play and how to play it. All he had to do was to move his hands. He felt that he had been empowered with the super-vision of a divine force.

Another time, he was playing at the Mahakal temple in Ujjain, for the Mahakaleshwar Utsav. It was around midnight when Panditji went on stage. Half an hour after he began playing, a strange thing happened. Suddenly, the birds sleeping on the trees around, woke up and started an orchestrated chirping. The twittering was not at all disturbing because it was going with the tempo of the *raag* Panditji was playing. The audience was surprised — rather overawed by this strange occurrence because this was hardly the hour for birds to wake up. Soon they started dropping twigs, leaves and flowers over the vast open-air stage and especially over Panditji.

A couple of months later Panditji was nominated for the Grammy. He still believes that the birds had become the communicators of God and were showering His blessings in the form of twigs and leaves. He believes that he received the Grammy because of the blessings of Mahakal.

Panditji believes in religious rituals. He feels that rituals bring people together spiritually, mentally and physically. They help in developing concentration of mind. Also through rituals people are able to express their faith in the Almighty.

He bows in front of the images of gods every morning, before starting his meals and before embarking on a journey. Through prayer he conveys his feelings to God. Prayer helps him in relieving the pain and anguish that sometimes swells up in his heart. He feels that prayer is the only means of gathering the cosmic energy and using it for a good cause. It helps him in getting answers when he is confused and prayers make him realize his mistakes. He also prays when he sees sufferings around him.

While exploring new passages in music he prays to Goddess Sarasvati. He admits that, "the Goddess then showers Her blessings on my soul and I get totally immersed in music." He continues, "I again stress that prayer fills me up with fresh breath and new ideas. I am then able to concentrate on my work and the results are always very encouraging."

To Panditji the word "faith" implies his endless love and devotion for the Almighty and the people around him. In return he expects them to love him and care for him. He feels that faith makes him a better and a stronger person.

Once a time did come in his life when his faith in God was shaken and he was angry with God. He admits, "Yes, my faith has been tested and tested very hard. I had been extremely angry with God when my eleven-year-old foster daughter lost her battle to death. I never expected that God would snatch her from us so soon. My wife had named her Surabhi (*sur* means a musical note and *surabhi* means the scent of the musical note). We could experience God smiling when

Padma Bhatt with foster daughter Surabhi

With Asha Bhonsle

With an accompanist

she used to smile. She was very different from children of her age. She was very quiet, but one could see the light of life on her face. She was the very definition of innocence and a picture of selflessness. She had taught all of us how to be happy in all circumstances. She died having no sign of pain or complaint on her face. We could see her fighting for every breath. We were able to see some force pulling her away from us. I was furious because my prayers to God went unheard. I couldn't see my Surabhi being silenced forever. I wanted to ask God why he was doing so. Was this the destiny of our child who had not even seen what the world was like? I wanted to give her all the happiness and joy of the world but now I could give her nothing except a flood of tears and a white cloth which adorned her during the last rites. This couldn't be her end and it surely is not. It took me a few days and nights to accept the cruel fact that she was not with us. I talked to myself and got an answer — that God had taken her because he loved her more than us. God never made my Surabhi go through the pain, agony and suffering which we so often see around us. Then I realized that she had attained *moksha*. She was free from the birth and death cycle and all the earthly bondages. It was then that I apologized to God. I hope I have been forgiven. I thank the Almighty who has given me and my family members the strength to bear the untimely loss", he says.

It so happened that just a couple of days after Surabhi's death Panditji had to go to Bangalore for a concert. This concert had been planned one year in advance. The tickets had been sold out and a lot spent on publicity. So Panditji was in a fix, whether to go or not to go. Ultimately he decided to go but was not sure whether he would be able to perform. He recalls, "It was time for me to begin the performance. I was enveloped in grief and with trembling hands I picked up my instrument and my feet took me to the stage. I remembered Surabhi and began my performance. It took me some time to find my flow but I realized that some force was making me play on. I felt that I was able to express my feelings through my instrument. There was a complete flow of ideas from my heart to my hands. I felt that I was reaching the souls and minds of each and everyone sitting in the Hall and I was telling them about my longing for my Surabhi. My heart that had been heavy was now light and I experienced my body and soul coming out of the shell of grief. I could sense that I was transformed into a much better and stronger human being. I could feel Surabhi's presence beside me and I could visualize her smiling at my achievement. I acknowledged God's blessings being showered on me. Creativity never stops. Even death cannot stop it."

Leading the Manganiars into the hearts of city dwellers

Panditji believes that God has assigned to him the task of spreading peace and harmony through music — and he is totally committed to the task. The cadence of his music gives peace even to those who do not understand the technicalities of classical music.

Happy moments with Pt. Ravi Shankar and Sukanya Shankar

Panditji, wants his listeners to sink into the deep currents of Indian classical music and flow along its fanciful waves to an experience of paradise where malice, envy, greed and hatred do not exist. Through music he wants to awaken in man feelings of

kindness and compassion. He wants his music to bring peace, joy, happiness and solace to man, so that he may in turn elevate society.

In a stress-ridden urbanite world, Panditji's music is a tentative foray into the world of spiritualism. It is a stress-reliever. It not only helps one to look inwards, but also creates a sense of equanimity. It energizes the individual to meet the challenges ahead. Thus he has gone a long way in setting up the trend for therapeutic classical music.

Glossary

Alap — The beginning of a musical composition. It is a slow beatless expansion of the *raag* in which the musician develops the delicate and intricate nuances of the *raag*. He gives a general and total impression of the *raag*, its nature and flow through the *saptak*. Through the *alap* the listeners is familiarized with the phrases that would follow in the composition section along with the beats. The listener thus gets immersed into the purest *raag* mood.

Andolan — A free-swinging note that also allows the sounding of a higher note. It also involves the use of a mild *meend*.

Bhakti — A devotional, spiritual, religious character.

Dhaivat — Sixth scale step of the seven-tone scale in ascending order

Gamak — A melodic embellishment which involves the sounding of a particular note along with its adjacent notes through *meend* at a high speed.

Guru — Spiritual guide

Jhala — Third part of the rendition of a *raag*. It is characterized by increasing speed and excitement ending with a climax.

Kalyug — One of the four ages of the world in mythology, viz., *Satyug, Tretayug, Dvaparyug* and *Kalyug* (the present age).

Krishna — Lord Krishna is the eighth incarnation of Vishnu. He is often represented as a dark and handsome youth, playing the flute.

Meend — An embellishment which characterizes the sliding from one note to another, connecting their sounds, using microtones.

Maharaja — The King.

Mohani — Enchantment.

Pakad — A short section of a particular *raag* which embodies its characteristics and distinguishes it from any other *raag*.

Parampara — Tradition

Raag — The melodic basis of Indian Classical music. Each *raag* has its own definite melodic qualities and emotional impact upon which the musicians improvise.

Raja — King

Saval Jawab Session — A kind of question and answer dialogue between the main instrument and the drum.

Saptak — Seven notes (*shuddha svaras*) of the octave: *shadaja, rishaba, gandhara, madhya, panchama, dhaivata, nishada,* abbreviated as *sa, ri, ga, ma, pa, dha, ni*

Shishya — Disciple

Shruti — Microtones; the twenty-two intervals used within an octave.

Swara — Tone of a definite pitch.

Tansen — An eminent singer at Akbar's Court.

Talim — Instruction, training.

Vilambit — Slow

Vishwa — World.

Major Awards

S.No.	Awards	Year	City
1.	Sur Mani	1970	Mumbai
2.	Tantree Samrat	1981	Chandigarh
3.	Honorary Citizenship of State of USA	1989	Maryland (U.S.A.)
4.	Honorary Citizenship of Canada	1990	Toronto (Canada)
5.	Mewar Foundation Award	1990	Udaipur
6.	Mahakal Samman	1992	Ujjain
7.	Swar Shiromani	1993	Jaipur
8.	The Grammy Award (World's Highest Music Award)	1994	New York (USA)
9.	State Honour by the then Chief Minister of Rajasthan Shri Bhairon Singh Shekhawat (Rs. 1,00,000 cash Award)	1994	Jaipur
10.	Connect Award	1995	New Delhi
11.	Tantree Award	1995	Mumbai
12.	Tantree Samrat	1995	Chandigarh
13.	Rajasthan Shree	1996	Jaipur
14.	Musical Scientist Award	1996	Bangalore
15.	Australian Title (Most appealing Slide player of the planet)	1998	Sydney
16.	"Bharat Jyoti" Award	1999	New York
17.	Sangeet Natak Academy Award	1999	New Delhi
18.	Rajiv Gandhi Rashtriya Ekta Award	2001	New Delhi
19.	Padma Shree	2002	New Delhi

Dearest to my heart

Receiving the Sangeet Natak Academy Award
in 1999 from the then
President of India Shri K.R. Narayanan

The then President of India Shri K.R. Narayanan,
presenting the Padma Sri award to Pt. Vishwa Mohan Bhatt

I won them all!